Read Right!

COACHING YOUR CHILD TO EXCELLENCE IN READING

Dee Tadlock, Ph.D., with Rhonda Stone

McGraw·Hill

New York   Chicago   San Francisco   Lisbon   London   Madrid   Mexico City
Milan   New Delhi   San Juan   Seoul   Singapore   Sydney   Toronto

Library of Congress Cataloging-in-Publication Data

Tadlock, Dee.
   Read right : coaching your child to excellence in reading / Dee Tadlock with
Rhonda Stone.—1st ed.
       p.   cm.
   Includes bibliographical references and index.
   ISBN 0-07-145510-8
   1. Reading (Early childhood)   2. Reading—Parent participation.   I. Stone,
Rhonda.   II. Title.

   LB1139.5.R43T33   2005
   372.4—dc22   2005003487

2 3 4 5 6 7 8 9 0   DOC/DOC   0 9 8 7 6 5

ISBN 0-07-145510-8

McGraw-Hill books are available at special quantity discounts to use as premiums and
sales promotions, or for use in corporate training programs. For more information, please
write to the Director of Special Sales, Professional Publishing, McGraw-Hill, Two Penn
Plaza, New York, NY 10121-2298. Or contact your local bookstore.

This book is printed on acid-free paper.

To my son . . . and all children and adults who would like to be able to read with excellence

Contents

Foreword

A wealth of research is expanding our understanding of the neurophysiology and neuroanatomy of structures underlying speech and language development and clinical disorders, such as stuttering, autism spectrum disorders, specific language learning disabilities, and more. These studies are driving the development of a wide variety of more effective and efficient interventions to improve patient diagnosis and outcome. This is an exciting time for brain research. We are actually beginning to study the plasticity of the brain, the neural networks that make learning possible, and the genes that control that plasticity.

In the Childrens Brain Center here at Childrens Hospital Los Angeles, we are preparing to study how children develop effective language. These studies will involve learning styles, strengths, and limitations in normal children and children with neurologic deficits (from abnormal development and acquired through injury or disease). Research within these programs will examine neural network plasticity. We will find out whether neural network disruption can benefit from appropriately timed stimulation of the systems associated with language. The investigators for these programs will work with pediatric neurologists, pediatric neuropsychologists, and pediatric neuroradiologists dedicated to functional imaging of the brain in order to understand how language, speech, and reading really work.

However, for the large number of children and adults without specific impediments to language, speech, and reading development, but who are unable to read efficiently, the straightforward strategies detailed in Dr. Tadlock's book form an effective guide to parents and educators that illuminates the way for those frustrated by the side steps of other educational systems. Over the years I have watched the development of Dr. Tadlock's methods and have seen astonishing growth in the numbers of children and adults who became efficient readers under her guidance. I have a very personal example of the effectiveness of these methods.

My adult son became a functional reader for the first time in his life as a result of the techniques presented in this book. He wasn't a child when he learned to read, though I wish he had been. He was a middle-aged adult, whose life had already been shaped by many years of struggling with learning. Through the years, my family investigated and implemented one intervention after another to help my son. Just as many, many families before and after us have experienced, the interventions did little to help him. Members of my family even became actively involved in state and federal legislation to protect the rights and interests of children in similar situations—children with significant learning problems.

Several years ago, my brother asked my son if he would be interested in being tutored by long-distance telephone with methodology developed by his wife, Dr. Tadlock. My son was willing. I was intrigued by my son's relatively quick progress with Dr. Tadlock's highly structured methodology and couldn't help but wonder what she had stumbled upon. From this book, I now understand that she didn't "stumble upon" anything.

As I read these pages from cover to cover, I found the ideas to be remarkably consistent with knowledge of how brains function and the emerging understanding of the brain's wondrous and natural plasticity. With a foundation of neuroscience, Dr. Tadlock provides a plausible framework to explain mysteries that have stumped the reading field for decades.

I finally understand why this methodology worked to help my son when all other conventional approaches failed. Professionally, I am intrigued and impressed by her discoveries and am pleased to share with you that my son now reads high-school level material with ease and comfort. The effect on his life is extremely impressive.

There are important ideas between the covers of this book. Parents of young children will benefit from them, as will people of all ages with reading difficulties. I believe that it is valuable for both parents and science that Dr. Tadlock has decided to share her discoveries.

—Floyd Gilles, M.D.
Head, Childrens Brain Center, Childrens Hospital Los Angeles
Burton E. Green Professor of Pediatric Neuropathology
Childrens Hospital Los Angeles
Professor of Neuropathology, Neurosurgery, and Neurology
Keck School of Medicine, University of Southern California, Los Angeles

Acknowledgments

The list of individuals who have contributed to the web of events that made this book possible is long: first and foremost, my son, whose reading problems all those years ago caused me to take that first tentative step on a path of discovery; professional colleagues and friends like Jan Swinton, Rita Smilkstein, and others whose willingness to discuss my thinking and offer questions and insights shaped the direction I would take; my former husband, Larry Tadlock, who was on the path with me for most of the journey, lending support in countless ways; my present husband, Lee Gilles, who saw the vision and brought the business expertise required to establish a company dedicated to the mission of eliminating reading problems; the entire staff of READ RIGHT® Systems, Inc., who work daily to actualize the mission; our veteran READ RIGHT consultants Jason Campbell, Justin McIntosh, Jon Yunker, Barbara Kehayes, my son Shane Tadlock, Doug Fadness, and James Zion, who not only train tutors superbly but also provide a continuous stream of improvement suggestions; my son Kyle Tadlock, who has a gift for looking at complex systems, extracting the core elements, and succinctly describing how they operate and how they contribute to the whole—his work is reflected throughout this book and has made replication of our system possible; Rod Riggenbaugh, who manages our company's information systems with more patience than one would deem possible; our CEO, Tom Brown, who has valiantly protected me from competing interests to carve out the time to complete the book; the many educators who have seen the transformative power of the interactive constructivist view of reading, have been awed by the power of the brain to change itself, and are inspired to do what they can to transform all poor readers into excellent ones; the clients who have become friends and partners in working to eliminate reading problems for all children by sharing their experiences with the interactive constructivist methodology at conferences and in many other ways—Sharon Schmitt, Bob McLaughlin, Mary Cook, Melinda Reeves, Jo Woodruff, Jennifer Smurthwaite, Ruth Pettitt, Jeff Rayburn, Mervina Sturgeon, Tammy Summers, Faye Fulton, Jennifer Miller, Bonnie Varner, Kathy Christiansen, Marsha Hanson, Mike Bumgartner, Dave Cotlove, and many others; my agent, Jeff Kleinman, and editors Meg Leder and Natasha Graf, of McGraw-Hill, who made the book possible through their confidence in its worth; Rhonda Stone, whose contribution to this book was more than I had any right to expect; and finally, my parents, who taught me to always question and discover for myself.

Introduction

It was six men of Indostan
To learning much inclined,
Who went to see the Elephant
(Though all of them were blind),
That each by observation
Might satisfy his mind . . .
　　　　　—from a poem by John Godfrey Saxe, 1816–1887

In this East Indian fable, six blind men sought to answer the question: What is an elephant? Each focused on a single aspect of the huge creature. As a result, the elephant was described as being like a wall by the man who felt the side of the elephant, like a spear by the one who touched the tusk, and like a snake by the one who examined the trunk. The blind man who felt the leg said an elephant was like a tree, and the one who slid his hands down the tail insisted it was like a rope. The man who felt the ear "knew" the others were wrong. He said the elephant was like a fan. The moral of the fable: one cannot understand the whole of something by focusing only on its parts.

Reading is literacy's proverbial "elephant." It is complex, dynamic, and easily misunderstood if one or a few of its many "parts" are assumed to be representative of the whole. For the past decade, the field of reading has been dominated by the belief—recurring throughout its history—that reading development requires explicit, systematic instruction in a narrow set of specific skills. If you have children in school, you are probably familiar with these skills: phonemic awareness (knowing that spoken words are formed by stringing individual sounds together), phonics (linking alphabetic letters to the sounds of spoken words), vocabulary (individual words for which you know the meaning), fluency (smooth, uninterrupted reading), and comprehension (understanding an author's message).

The belief that these skills must be taught separately contradicts important discoveries made in the 1960s about young children who taught themselves to read. The four- and five-year-olds who were studied had virtually no explicit, systematic instruction in phonemic awareness, phonics, vocabulary, fluency, or comprehension, yet they figured out how to read all by themselves. Such children read efficiently and effectively—and they remain excellent readers for life. We talk more about the studies in Chapter 1.

Read Right: Coaching Your Child to Excellence in Reading presents a new view of what is required for excellent reading development. The new view is grounded in a recent explosion of knowledge related to how brains function and what is known and accepted about how we all learn processes (how to walk, talk, ride a bicycle, and so on).

In this book you are invited to examine reading through a whole new set of eyes—through eyes that understand that *passage reading* (reading sentences and paragraphs of text) is not about each and every word or a set of skills. Rather, passage reading is about all of the complex, dynamic, and integrated brain systems that must work together to give life and meaning to the ideas communicated by authors.

This new view is articulated and introduced for the first time in the following pages to help parents like you coach preschool-age children into constructing their own excellent reading ability. Through new understanding of what all excellent readers do when they read passages of text, you can help your children prepare for reading development and help them *read right* for a lifetime.

"Every man who knows how to read has it in his power to magnify himself, to multiply the ways he exists, to make his life full, significant, and interesting."

—Aldous Huxley

PART I

Reading Is Not "Taught"

Buckle your seat belt! This section is guaranteed to challenge your current beliefs about reading and will introduce the idea that reading ability is not "taught." In the following pages, we will present the view that passage reading is not simply the result of the application of a specific set of explicit skills. Rather, it is a complex neurobiological process performed by the brain that must be "figured out" by every young reader implicitly—or below the level of consciousness. Remember the word implicit. You will see it often throughout this book. Because reading operates implicitly, no one has access to or control over what must be done to make reading happen. Too often, when we, as well-meaning parents and educators, attempt to teach young children to read, we unintentionally cause some children's brains to go down "the wrong path" in figuring out the complex process. Faulty guidance and instruction, not brain differences, therefore, are likely the primary reason that so many otherwise bright and capable children and adults have reading problems. Developing an understanding of what we actually do when we read with excellence and how brains learn will help you influence your child's reading development in a positive and appropriate way.

PART 1

Reading Is Not "Taught"

1

Learning from Children Who Teach Themselves to Read

Josie is barely four years old. In her family's living room, she has just finished constructing a ring of books. She bunny hops over Eric Carle's *The Hungry Caterpillar*, plops onto her knees in the center of the ring, and scans the covers, looking for just the right book. She finds her favorite, *Frog and Toad Are Friends*, and cracks it open. Four-year-old Josie begins to read.

Josie isn't even in kindergarten yet—so, who taught her to read? Ask her parents, and they shrug, "No one." Adds her mother, "I read to her a lot, and she just picked it up!"

Nestled next to moms and dads, brothers and sisters, grandparents and family friends, "Josie" represents thousands of children who each year develop reading skills apart from any formal instruction and before they start school. It can be done, it has been done, and you can help your child do it too. Since the 1950s, these children have been studied by different researchers who haven't yet figured out how they do it. Within these pages, the mystery is solved!

Understanding the mystery of how young children like Josie teach themselves to read has the potential to benefit every child who will one day become a reader. This important knowledge will help *you* duplicate the necessary conditions in your own home, provide you with important information about what truly drives the development of reading ability, and help you guide your preschool-age child into his or her own reading development. Children who figure out how to read with excellence on their own are unlikely to *ever* develop a reading problem.

An Early Reader Learns to Read

I was one of those kids who teach themselves to read. When I was young, my mother consistently read to my older brother and me from picture books and children's classics such as *The Adventures of Tom Sawyer, Mrs. Wiggs of the Cabbage Patch, Black Beauty*, and others. Like nearly all kids who are read to often, we had our favorite books that we wanted to hear over and over again. My mother almost always complied with our redundant requests, in part because she enjoyed the stories, too!

So, from an early age, I was introduced to the rich language and ideas in books and the joys of good stories. My partners on the journey were family members I loved dearly. From them I learned to value reading.

My brother learned to read before I did. When I was five and he was seven, he introduced me to the excitement and fun of comic books. The supply was limited in our household, so he often read the same comic to me again and again. Left at home while my brother went to school, I desperately wanted to read those comics. I'd pull them out and study the pictures, look at the print on the page, and wish I could re-create the stories, eagerly anticipating the next time my brother would read to me. To this day, I don't recall exactly what I did to figure out how to read the comic books; I recall only how much I wanted to be able to read to them.

I still remember the day I was able to read my first comic book by myself—with absolutely no formal reading instruction from my brother or any adult. It was so exciting to experience stories coming to life in my mind. I kept reading on my own and became increasingly eager to show my brother what I could do. At our next comic book session, when I announced that I wanted to read to him, he was skeptical. With a smirk, he handed me a comic book.

He was shocked by what happened next. I read with understanding, ease, and comfort. My brother was simultaneously surprised and proud of his little sister. Because of my September birthday, I was still two school years away from first grade when I started reading. (Preschools and kindergartens were few and far between in the late 1940s, so my formal education would not start until first grade.) Not long after I proved to my brother that I could read, we had a house full of company, including several small children. Mom asked my brother to read to the little kids in order to quiet them down. His response: "Tell Dee to do it."

Mom responded, "Don't be silly. She can't read!"

Eager to prove her wrong, my brother ran to the bedroom for a comic book, brought it out, and said, "Yes she can. Show her, Dee."

You can imagine what happened next. I read, and my mother was amazed at my ability to do so with ease and comfort.

Of course, I had no idea how I taught myself to read. In fact, even as a graduate student specializing in reading, I didn't have a clue how it could be possible. The idea wasn't even a glimmer in my mind until a fateful event: the development of my own son's significant reading problem. That crisis led to more than twenty years of work and research with struggling readers of all ages. Working with them has led to my firm belief that virtually all children *can* teach themselves to read—and they are much better off when they do.

Raising a Son with a Reading Problem

By the time I had finished the course work for my Ph.D. in education with an emphasis in reading and passed the comprehensive exams, my son was just entering first grade. He was a social and bright child with a highly developed vocabulary. We had no concerns about his ability to do well; however, after several months, it became clear that he had a reading problem.

My first reaction was shock. That was supposed to happen to other people's children, not mine. I checked through all the characteristics that are supposed to be prophetic of reading problems, and none of them fit. My son had excellent command of language and a wealth of childhood experiences to draw from, was read to a great deal from the time he was small, and so on—all characteristics considered to this day to be foundational to reading development. Nonetheless, there he was, engaged in a day-to-day struggle with reading.

My second reaction: "Isn't he lucky to have a reading specialist for a mom?" How naive I was! I had great expectations about how I was going to solve his reading problem because I was an expert in reading. Someday, I thought, when he was old enough to understand, I'd tell him what a wonderful thing I'd done, and he'd be grateful.

But it didn't turn out that way. I worked diligently with my son, using all the latest research and methodologies I'd learned in graduate school, and yet, there was no improvement in his ability to read. I was dismayed. Despite my extreme motivation to help him and his willingness to work hard, we got nowhere. My son was begging for help, saying things such as: "I've got to learn to read, Mom! Uncle Bill reads; Aunt Linda reads; you and Dad read. Everybody reads. Why can't I?" I lay awake at night trying to think of other approaches, but I was out of ideas. My son was still struggling with reading. I felt a sense of panic. I didn't know what else I could do.

Meanwhile, my son's first-grade teacher was having the same lack of results. She tried all the strategies teachers are taught to use when a child struggles with reading—focusing on phonics and sight words, guided practice in blending sounds, timed reading sessions to encourage him to identify words more quickly, and so on. Despite her hard work and professional competence, she couldn't help him either.

Looking for Answers

Finally, I was called to a meeting at school to determine how my son could be best served. Based on information provided through testing and by my son's teacher, the school psychologist suggested additional testing to see if he was "learning-disabled" and eligible for a special program in a school across town. I inquired about the instructional program in the school to which he would be bussed and was invited to visit. There, I observed extremely competent educators doing the same things his classroom teacher and I had already done separately and thoroughly with no success. It didn't make sense to me to continue to do the same old things and expect to get different results. I respectfully declined the program. I didn't want my son bussed across town, away from the teacher, friends, and brother he loved, to attend a program unlikely to work because there was nothing new being offered. When I refused the special program, the principal asked me to sign a waiver stating that the school was no longer accountable for my son's reading instruction.

Signing that waiver was a crucial turning point in my life. Essentially, I was declaring publicly that I alone in the world was responsible for my son's future success in reading, and yet, I had convincingly demonstrated that I hadn't a notion of how to help him. All I knew was that both the school and I had exhausted the current pool of knowledge about how to help a child with a reading problem, and he still couldn't read.

I went home with a heavy heart to think about it. Even though I had no idea how to proceed, I knew that there was absolutely nothing wrong with my child. He was a bright, social boy who did well in school—well with everything not directly connected to reading.

Rather than redouble my efforts, I stopped working with my son. I believe strongly that when you attempt to teach someone, your method ought to have a chance of working. I feared that muddling around with teaching techniques that yielded no benefit might damage my son's self-esteem, and in truth, it already had. The little boy who had once eagerly looked forward to school no longer wanted to go. He began to invent illnesses with the hope of staying home. His self-confidence eroded, until ultimately, he uttered the words that broke my heart: "I'm too stupid to do it, Mom."

A Personal Revelation

Right around this time, I experienced a revelation. My upstairs neighbor was having a lot of trouble with her car. It was dying frequently and leaving her stranded, so she took it to a mechanic. When she got the car back from the mechanic, it died on the way home, leaving her stranded once again. She was furious. She came into my apartment ranting, "How can that guy say he's a mechanic? I can't believe it! He doesn't know how to fix cars! I've got to find a mechanic who knows what he's doing and get this car fixed once and for all!"

As she raved, lightbulbs started to blaze in my head. I recognized an analogy between her car and my son. She wasn't blaming the car. She wasn't complaining, "Oh dear. I have a car that is permanently disabled and can't be fixed." Instead, she was convinced that out there, somewhere, was the knowledge required to fix her car. Her job was to find the mechanic who had the knowledge to get the car fixed.

"Ah!" I thought. "My son isn't the problem—I simply haven't yet found the knowledge to help him. That doesn't mean the knowledge isn't out there. My job is to find it."

The encounter with my neighbor provided me with a direction in which to refocus my efforts and rekindled my hope. I promised my son I would leave no stone unturned in my quest to figure out why he was struggling to read. I didn't promise him a solution. I couldn't. I wasn't certain I would find one.

I began with an obvious question: What don't I know? That's a tough one. If you don't know what it is that you don't know, how can you possibly find it? I tackled the question by thinking once again of my neighbor's mechanic. What is it that a mechanic must know to be able to fix any automobile engine, no matter why it isn't operating properly? The answer: the mechanic has to know *exactly* what an automobile engine is doing when it operates efficiently and effectively. So, I reasoned, if I am going to find a way to fix my son's reading problem, I have to know what a brain does when it reads efficiently and effectively. And I must also understand how a brain learns a process, because reading, like any other "how to" activity such as walking, talking, or bicycle riding, is a process.

I was relieved to find a direction for proceeding, yet I was sobered by the realization that I was almost finished with my doctoral program in reading and didn't have an inkling about what the brain actually does when it reads, or what young readers must do to figure out the process. It wasn't that I had missed an important aspect of my training. The reality was and continues to be that no one has yet accurately defined what brains do when they read or how reading ability develops. My educational experiences put me in a peculiar position: I should have been able to teach my son to read, but I couldn't. I was left with two choices: I could accept defeat, or I could do everything in my power to figure out why the accepted methodologies didn't work and why my son couldn't learn to read. For my son, I chose to seek answers.

The Search for Knowledge to Help My Son

For the next three years, university and city libraries, with their rooms filled with books and journals, became my cocoon. I wasn't searching for a new way to teach reading. Rather, I sought understanding about the brain and the fundamental processes that must be involved in the act of reading. I found myself having to synthesize information from many different fields.

The one moment among many that stands out in my memories of the research years is the day I understood what a handful of now controversial reading theorists were saying about the differences between how reading is typically taught and how language is learned. In the 1970s and '80s, whole-language theorists pointed out that we don't teach children to understand language or speak by first focusing on the individual sounds of speech. On the contrary, verbal language is constructed by children implicitly through day-to-day interaction with adults and older children who speak to them. As children experience people talking to them, they make their own attempts to communicate through speech until they figure out the complex process of spoken language. They learn to speak as an integrated, interactive, implicit process grounded in the intent to communicate—not as a set of explicit skills that must be learned separately and sequentially.

If verbal language can't be taught separately and sequentially, why would anyone assume that printed language can? Yet, many contemporary reading specialists still believe reading must first be broken into separate puzzle pieces (identified as phonemic awareness, phonics, vocabulary, fluency, and comprehension), with the pieces taught separately and sequentially. The act of reading is finally accomplished through reassembly of the pieces.

From "aha"s like this, I learned to keep my mind open to new thinking. I didn't initially reject the old methodologies that I had been taught by reading professors, but I did try to set aside those ideas while I synthesized information from a variety of fields. Separating myself from old ideas made it possible for me to be open to new ways of interpreting information. I sought to answer two key questions:

1. What does the brain do when it reads well?
2. How does the brain learn a process?

I investigated current thinking in the fields of linguistics, language acquisition theory, information theory, communication theory, cognitive psychology, neurobiology, and neuropsychology. I was heavily influenced by the work of Jean Piaget, a world-renowned leader in the field of the development of intelligence, and Donald Hebb, a neuropsychologist who was the first to hypothesize that learning something new is reflected in physical brain changes.

Of the many studies I read, one of my favorites had to do with the brain's natural ability to adjust to significant changes in its visual field. In this now famous study of vision and perception, the subjects wore specially designed prism eyeglasses that caused the world to flip so that everything appeared upside down and backward. The people participating in the experiment had to wear these glasses twenty-four hours a day so that if they woke up at night, what appeared upright would still be down, and left would still be right. The research question posed was, Will the brain adjust and be able to function normally in this topsy-turvy environment?

The subjects took only a matter of weeks to accommodate and see the world right side up through the glasses. In order to do this, the brain had to totally adjust how it was interpreting the incoming visual messages. The researcher then removed the special glasses in order to test how long it would take the subjects to see the world normally without them. Without the glasses, the subjects saw the world topsy-turvy and upside down again because their brains were still compensating. This time, however, it was only a matter of days before the subjects' brains adjusted and saw the world right side up.

The power of the brain to adapt to a new environment amazed me and gave me hope that, given the right environment, a brain struggling with a serious reading problem might, indeed, adapt and overcome the problem.

A study in the area of language acquisition further demonstrated for me that the brain is well equipped to learn what it needs to learn and will do so automatically and unintentionally if the environment is right. In this experiment, researchers directed strangers to lean over infants in cribs and speak the same message to the babies. Each person, however, spoke the message in a different language, and only one spoke in the language used in the babies' homes. The researchers discovered that the infants responded vigorously to their native languages by kicking and squirming. The babies were responding to total strangers based only on the type of language spoken! These babies already had learned how to identify the sounds of their native tongues, and given their tender ages, such learning had to be subconscious. It had to happen because the babies on an implicit level understood that they must make sense of language in order to adapt and function successfully in their environments.

From the glasses, language, and other such experiments, I finally appreciated that the human brain is extremely adaptable and fully capable of doing what it needs to do in order to learn on an implicit or subconscious level. I also understood that the reading field has come to view reading as an act involving explicit skills that can be taught. Reading is not an explicit act! It is an implicit process. If it weren't for the amazing power of the brain to figure out how to perform processes, there would be no hope of correcting reading problems and guiding young children into excellence in reading.

Failures and Successes to Help the Brain Learn a Process

As I continued to read more and more research studies about brain functioning, I was increasingly awed and humbled by the capability of the brain to mold its own inner environment—the universe we create inside our heads as we interact with the world around us. How can the brain do this? When it sets out to learn a process, whether it be reading or bicycle riding, the brain does something remarkable all on its own:

1. It begins with a *clear understanding* of what it is trying to achieve.
2. It *anticipates* or *predicts* how to perform the process.

3. It makes an *attempt* based on its predictions.
4. It *compares* the results of the attempt with what it is seeking to achieve.
5. It *adjusts* the predictions based on a hypothesis of how to improve.
6. It *attempts* to do the process again.

This is how brains use anticipation, or a repetitive pattern of predictions, to make sense of how to perform any process—in other words, to create *meaningful* activity from that which has captured the brain's interest and attention. This respect for the power of the human brain to construct meaningful activity through interactions with the world became a key factor in all of my subsequent thinking on literacy and in the development of a new methodology for guiding children, teens, and adults into exceptional reading ability. It inspired me with the conviction that, in the right environment and with the right guidance, it is possible for children to "figure out" how to perform nearly any process—including reading. Adults don't need to be in control. Indeed, it is not possible to "teach" a child each little step in any learning process, because the brain has to implicitly construct its own learning. What every parent has to do instead is:

1. Provide the right kind of environment and guidance.
2. Then, stand back and let the child's brain do what it knows how to do subconsciously, naturally, and wonderfully—*anticipate, experiment,* and *learn!*

From the glasses experiment, I understood that if the brain possessed an accurate concept of what it was trying to achieve, it could achieve nearly anything. This caused me to believe that, if I could cause my son on an implicit level to understand that excellent reading must always make sense and feel comfortable, his subconscious brain would then begin to anticipate and experiment with how to make this kind of reading happen all on its own. As it conducted its myriad experiments, the brain would actually begin to change what it was doing when it read.

As I began to form new ideas, my son continued to struggle with reading. It was discouraging. On the one hand, I was dancing as fast as I could to unravel a mystery, and on the other, I had a son who was sinking deeper and deeper into a sea of negativity. In third grade, my son began to ask questions that caused me to worry that he was losing hope.

"Mom," he said, "if I can't read, will I be able to get a driver's license?" "If I can't keep up with my schoolwork, Mom, will they let me play football?"

At that point, his reading problem was pretty typical of children who are struggling to identify individual words. His reading was slow and laborious, with many pauses throughout. Although he didn't read for fun, he wasn't pushing books out of his life, either. I continued to read to him regularly. In the first two years of school, he was so bright and good in everything else that we hoped he'd pick up reading eventually. But it didn't happen. At home, he worked too long and too hard at his homework. We encouraged him to go outside and play with his friends, but he would shake his head and say, "No, I've got to work on this." He would say things like, "I don't want to be a top reader, Mom. I just want to be average." Finally, to ease the pressure he was putting on himself, we helped him decide to repeat the third grade. He was working so hard to make it in school that he wasn't a child anymore. He had become a full-time student!

Applying New Thinking to Eliminate Reading Problems

After three years of research, I emerged from my cocoon of libraries ready to apply new thinking with my son, who by then was in his second year of third grade. His self-esteem was shattered, he verbalized how stupid he thought he was, and he often cried because he didn't want to go to school and face a dozen failures every day. It was a horrible and broken situation for him and not much better for the rest of the family. It was heartbreaking to watch him sink deeper and deeper into despair as our efforts failed.

But, finally, I was armed with new ideas and ready to make a fresh attempt to help him. The new ideas constituted a complete shift in thinking about what is required for every child to become an excellent reader. The focus would not be on explicit "sounding out" and other word-identification strategies. Instead, the new focus would be on the consistent production of *excellence* with every single attempt that my son made at reading.

I worked with my son, refining the methodology I thought would work as we went along. I hoped for slow but steady improvement. To my utter shock and amazement, we didn't experience the mere incremental improvement that I expected. Rather, in just three months, my son and I celebrated the *total elimination* of his reading problem! After years of frustration, I could hardly believe that his reading problem could vanish in just a matter of months.

We were successful not because I taught my son a set of skills, but because I understood that, in the right environment, my son had to figure out for himself the complex process of passage reading. He had to do it by learning to hold himself accountable for producing reading that is excellent in every respect. Driven by strong intent to achieve excellence, his brain would engage in the implicit experiments needed to discover what makes reading happen. My job was to provide him with the right kind of environment as well as gentle, subtle guidance to help him get the job done. It was and continues to be a dramatically new idea for reading development and addressing reading problems.

Once my son's reading problem was eliminated, we got back the bright, inquisitive, smiling, confident child we had lost four years earlier. Over the next dozen years, I refined the methodology to reflect all that I had learned. We tested and perfected it with elementary, middle, and high school students; young adults in the junior college environment; and workplace adults with long histories of reading failure.

In 1991, my husband and I officially gave the methodology a name, READ RIGHT®, and cofounded a company to train tutors for schools and corporations in the United States, Canada, and China. Since that time, it has worked to improve the reading ability of more than twenty thousand children, teens, and adults, including special education students, students for whom English was not their native language, and other struggling readers. In that time, we have consistently observed students with long, painful histories of reading problems transform themselves into efficient and effective readers.

Not too long ago, the U.S. government considered any reading program to be effective that could deliver one grade level of improvement for every one hundred hours of tutoring or instruction. Since 1991, we have kept comprehensive records of virtually every person who was tutored with our methodology to address reading problems. Our records show that struggling readers of all ages and diverse backgrounds gained an average of one grade level of improvement for every *fourteen hours* of tutoring. At corporate sites and middle and high schools best at delivering the methodology, the rate of improvement was often one full grade of reading advancement for every *nine hours* of tutoring. Such results are rarely ever seen with struggling readers. It could be possible only if the new view accurately reflects what the brain needs to develop excellent reading ability. Amazing stories of individuals whose lives have been touched by the now patented READ RIGHT methodology are presented at the ends of chapters throughout this book.

This twenty-year record of success with struggling readers holds tremendous implications for parents and other adults working with preschool-age children who have not yet begun to read. It shows that there is a right way and a wrong way to work with developing readers and that the wrong way has the potential to cause significant numbers of children to go down the wrong path for reading. Putting it bluntly, the wrong path has the potential to lead to reading failure.

Blame Old Ideas About Reading, Not Children or Families

Reading failure, sadly, continues to be all too common. In 2004, the federal government estimated that twenty million children in the United States—approximately two children out of every five—continued to struggle with reading. It is a bleak statistic. Additionally, federal officials have stated that only one out of four children who have a reading problem after the age of nine will ever become an adequate reader.

There are inoculations for many life-threatening childhood diseases, but there is no inoculation for reading failure. Reading problems can be found in every type of home and under every type of circumstance, even in homes where parents spend hundreds of hours reading to their children.

Today, the reasons offered for widespread reading problems among children commonly include poor instructional practices by teachers, deficits in the students themselves, and challenges in the home or community environments. In other words, the blame lies with the teacher or the student or the family. To fix the reading problem, experts can only recommend that teachers try multiple methods of instruction in the hope that one or more will successfully connect with a child's particular learning style or successfully address an undefined learning problem.

The fault for widespread reading failure is not that of teachers, students, or their families. Rather, the fault lies with old and persistent ideas about reading and reading instruction that continue to dominate the reading field. In truth, the same old ideas have been rehashed, reorganized, and relabeled for the past two hundred years in an attempt to make the outdated ideas work for all children. The "same old ideas" identified by many reading theorists as fundamental skills to be taught are listed in Table 1.1.

Is knowledge of these skills really essential for reading development? It wasn't for Josie, introduced at the beginning of this chapter. Neither was such knowledge necessary for the more than two hundred early readers studied by Dolores Durkin of Columbia University and the University of Illinois. In the 1950s, Durkin began studying children in California and New York who entered school already able to read. Phonics and sounding out words were popular concepts in the 1960s. Durkin even authored several works on phonics. Eventually, however, she found that the hundreds of self-taught readers that she studied received virtually no informal, formal, or systematic instruction in any of the skills historically associated with reading. Like Josie's mother, the parents of

Table 1.1   Old Ideas About Skills That Must Be Taught

Skill	Abbreviated Definition
Alphabetics or Phonics	The ability to identify the letters of the alphabet, letter combinations, and associated sounds
Decoding	Sounding out words
Word Attack	The ability to identify new words from their "word parts"
Sight Words	Recognizing a word without having to use decoding or word-attack strategies
Vocabulary	The range of words known to an individual
Fluency	Smooth, undisrupted reading (assumed to be made possible by strong decoding, word-attack, and word-recognition skills)
Comprehension	The ability to understand what is being read

these children did not know how their children became readers. What Durkin did find, however, were four common characteristics of these children and their home environments:

1. Frequent exposure of the children to many kinds of books,
   including alphabet books, simple stories, and more complex works of literature.
2. Determined children who had an extreme curiosity about
   reading and an almost insatiable desire to figure out the
   process.
3. Inquisitive children who frequently asked that the same
   stories be read to them again and again.
4. Readily available assistance from older readers to answer
   the children's many questions about the stories in books
   and to fulfill their requests.

Sound familiar? It sounds a lot like me and my family
when I was a child trying to figure out the reading process! I
suspect that these four characteristics will stir memories in
nearly every self-taught reader. They are characteristics that
can be duplicated by every family. As you read the four characteristics, did you notice that they bear little resemblance to
the elements commonly accepted by the reading field as essential to reading instruction?

New ideas are needed in the reading field because the old
ideas have never worked to ensure that *nearly every child*
becomes an excellent reader. If the children studied by Durkin
could figure out the passage reading process for themselves,
it stands to reason that—given the right environment and
guidance—nearly every child could figure out the process.

The Interactive Constructivist
View of Reading

A new view of reading and reading development, called the
interactive constructivist view, is presented in this book. It is
grounded in what is known and accepted about the formation

of neural networks in the brain to guide processes, as well as in the work of the highly regarded learning theorist Jean Piaget. Piaget's background was not in reading. Instead, his background was in the development of intelligence.

Piaget's work in combination with recent research from the field of brain science suggest what it is that brains need in order to develop excellence for the complex process of passage reading. Rather than constructing neural networks for the simplistic and linear function of sounding out or identifying words, the brain must construct neural circuitry for the much more complex and interactive act of passage reading. Simply stated, the quality of a child's reading ability depends wholly upon *how* the child first learns to read! Did the child construct neural circuitry designed to perform simplistic word-by-word reading, or did the child construct neural circuitry to do whatever is necessary to produce reading that always makes sense, feels comfortable, and seems like natural, conversational speech—the essence of truly excellent passage reading? See the difference?

From a new understanding of how brains form neural networks to guide processes and Piaget's work with children and the development of intelligence, it is fairly easy to figure out how all young children teach themselves to read.

You Are Your Child's Most Important Coach

As a parent, you are your child's first and most important coach, and as such, you are able to influence your child into excellent reading ability. Parents have been doing so without knowing exactly how for years. Now, for the first time, you can see precisely how the process works and what you can do to make it happen for your child.

Before we explore the techniques necessary to help children acquire this life-shaping ability, it is essential that you understand two things. First, if children as young as two, three, and four can teach themselves to read, your child can figure it out, too. This important concept may be hard for many people to accept, given the complexity of the passage-reading process. Be patient, and don't be intimidated by the task! Keep a picture in your mind of those two-, three-, and four-year-olds who taught themselves. If they can easily and successfully figure it out for themselves, your child can, too! The key is to keep it simple and get out of your child's way as much as you can. If you apply the techniques appropriately as they are presented in Chapters 4 through 7, your child likely will figure out the reading process for herself.

Second, the primary cause of reading problems is a faulty sense that reading is about identifying each and every word on the page. Any suggestion to children that they "sound out" a word or use other strategies that keep them hyperfocused on reading word by word has the potential to cause the child's brain to go down the wrong path. It is essential that you, as your child's most important coach, have a basic understanding of how the brain *reads*, as well as how the brain *learns*. These all-important issues are explained for you in the simplest of terms in Chapters 2 and 3. Read these chapters, study them, and do not move on to the how-to chapters (Part II) until you have a basic understanding of what they are attempting to communicate. Chapters 4 through 7 explain specific coaching techniques you can use with your child. Chapter 8 addresses the authentic barriers to reading development, and in Chapter 9, the book concludes with a discussion of what you might expect when your child starts school.

Children's success in reading depends wholly on the quality of the neural circuitry they will construct in their brains to guide the process of reading. In the same way, for you to be an effective reading coach, you need to construct neural circuitry in your own brain for coaching your child's reading activities. It is for this reason that you need to read, study, and experiment with the techniques provided in this book, while being ever mindful of using the techniques appropriately.

Success Story: Five-Year-Old Friends Become Avid Readers

The director of a community development organization shared the following story with me. He had obtained grant funding to place a READ RIGHT tutoring program at an area middle school. As part of the grant agreement, he employed the program's reading tutors to work with adults after school hours at another location. Largely out of curiosity, the director began to take his five-year-old granddaughter and a young friend of hers to the after-hours program two to three days a week.

The girls worked with the tutors alongside struggling teen and adult readers. Within three months, both girls were beginning to read, and within six months, both five-year-olds were avid readers, reading with excellence. At the same time, the director watched as middle school children and adults eliminated reading problems that had persisted for years. As you can imagine, this director is now a huge believer in the power of the new view of reading and the methodology developed to reflect it.

2

Understanding How Excellent Readers Read

I still remember what it was like to be in first grade and already know how to read. It was satisfying to be able to efficiently complete work sheets and comfortably read the simple books we were given in class. Yet, I remember feeling surprised that my classmates struggled with both activities. I had never read the way my peers read: by slowly and laboriously sounding out words (decoding). I had always simply read to know the story. From the beginning, I was an excellent reader. Because I had never been taught to be a decoder, I never focused on the words.

Why Decoding Is Different from Passage Reading

How, you might think, is it possible for any child to read with excellence when the child has had no experience whatsoever with decoding words? Simple. Decoding is not the same cognitive act as passage reading. Each requires significantly different activity in the brain. As counterintuitive as it may sound, a student who becomes proficient at identifying individual words will not necessarily become an excellent reader. The following two activities will help you understand this point.

Activity: Vowel-Less Words

Read these English words from which the vowels have been removed:

lttl

th

t

wnt

th

grl

str

With the vowels missing, was the list easy or difficult to read? Are you confident that you identified each word correctly?

Now try this:

Th lttl grl wnt t th str.

Is the second arrangement easier to read? Virtually everyone who has done this exercise reports that the second arrangement is much easier. Why? If efficient reading is nothing more than the ability to identify words quickly and easily, both tasks would be identical for the brain. But they aren't. The incomplete words presented in a random list are more difficult to read than the same words presented in a meaningful sentence—"The little girl went to the store." Clearly, word identification and passage reading are different cognitive acts.

Activity: Scrambled Words

The following activity is another demonstration that individual word identification and passage reading are different cognitive acts. Read the next sentence:

I beneficial read the to task presented be complex to
in on hope the discovering to in excellent cognitive

> *will information your how chapter become of you this*
> *an learning child help reader.*

The first thing you probably noticed about this activity is that your brain didn't like doing it. The brain is the organ of the body that is specifically responsible for making sense of everything around us. It probably didn't take long for your brain to realize that it couldn't easily and efficiently make sense of this paragraph. You may have kept reading, plodding through; you may have attempted to rearrange the words so the paragraph would make sense; or you may have simply quit reading. When the brain is put in a situation in which it cannot make sense, it no longer wants to participate.

Let's see if your brain likes this better:

> *I hope the information presented in this chapter on*
> *the complex cognitive task of learning to read will be*
> *beneficial to you in discovering how to help your child*
> *become an excellent reader.*

Think about the speed at which you read the two sentences. Each was composed of the same words. Why should you be able to read the same words faster if they are arranged in a meaningful sentence rather than randomly presented? If passage reading resulted from accurately and rapidly identifying each individual word, wouldn't the speed at which you can read these two sentences be nearly identical? Yet, most people report that they were able to read the meaningful sentence faster. From this exercise, all of us should be able to conclude that the brain is doing something other than simply identifying words as it reads.

Limitations to Memory

Why doesn't the brain read by identifying every word on the page? It seems like the simplest and most likely approach. The answer: all human brains have limitations as to the amount of information they can hold in short-term memory. These limitations make it difficult if not impossible to understand the text if you read to identify the sounds of speech (decoding) or individual words (sight words). For just a moment, let's experience how a pure decoder reads.

Activity: A Decoded Sentence

Decode the following sentence aloud, replacing the dashes with a brief pause. After you sound out all the parts of a word, say it, and then sound out the next one, and so on. This is the way first graders typically are taught to read if they cannot immediately identify the words!

Th–e y–e–ll–ow b–a–ll–oo–n w–i–ll ex–p–l–o–de wh–e–n i–t g–e–t–s t–oo b–i–g.

Such reading poses a significant challenge to the limitations of working memory (also called short-term memory). Scientists have determined that working memory doesn't have much capacity. On average it can hold only seven bits of information at a time—plus or minus two. A child who reads purely through decoding is confronted with the dilemma of too many bits of information that the brain must retain and assemble. The sentence in the preceding activity has at least thirty-eight bits of information, if each letter is sounded out separately. With decoding as the primary reading strategy, these bits of information have to be reassembled one by one in left-to-right sequential order to make sense of the sentence. However, by the time you finish sounding out the first three words (Th–e y–e–ll–ow b–a–ll–oo–n . . .), you have already exceeded the capacity of working memory! Like a computer program that has reached its capacity, a pure decoder will have to clear this information from memory in order to create space for what is yet to come.

The same working memory limitations impede understanding when readers read by identifying each and every word as a sight word. The following activity will help you experience what it is like to read—one—word—at—a—time.

Activity: Reading to Identify Words

Focus visually in a purposeful way on the first word in the following sentence and then say the word. Pause and then focus visually on the next word, say that word, and then pause again. Don't decode—just say each word. A cautionary note: your brain will be tempted to move ahead quickly as it seeks to read for understanding. Force yourself to focus on every word:

> *If—your—brain—always—reads—to—identify—
> words—rather—than—to—construct—the—
> author's—intended—message,—you—would—
> probably—avoid—doing—it.*

Not a very satisfying experience, is it? Did you get a sense of what we are asking young children to do when we direct them to focus on individual words rather than the *meaning* an author is attempting to convey? In language, meaning comes from multiple words strung together to represent a *single idea*—not from any one word in isolation! It is, therefore, easier for the brain to process ideas that involve many words than to process individual sounds or individual words. Through the identification of ideas, the brain can overcome the capacity limitations of short-term memory.

Reading to Identify Words Versus Reading from Meaning

The ideas expressed by authors (their intended meaning) provide the framework and support for the process of passage reading. Excellent readers read *from meaning*. They ground reading in what they already know. This is not to be confused with the skills-based and whole-language view that we read *for meaning*. The two views are significantly different. Reading *for* meaning suggests that you come to the meaning by identifying and adding up all of the individual words. Reading *from* meaning contends that the process can't happen unless you start, at the moment that you begin to read, by linking ideas in your mind with the ideas an author intends to convey.

Activity: A Bit of Free Verse

This activity demonstrates the difference between reading "for meaning" and reading "from meaning." Read the following verse:

> *With hocked gems financing him*
> *Our hero bravely defied all scornful laughter*
> *That tried to prevent his scheme*
> *Your eyes deceive he had said*
> *An egg not a table correctly typifies this unexplored planet*
> *Now three sturdy sisters sought proof*
> *Forcing along sometimes through calm vastness*
> *Yet more often over turbulent peaks and valleys*
> *Days become weeks*
> *As many doubters spread fearful rumors about the edge*
> *At last from somewhere welcome winged creatures appeared*
> *Signifying momentous success*
>
> —from a research article by
> D. J. Dooling and R. Lachman, 1971

Although every one of the individual words is easily identifiable, this passage is difficult for most people to understand. Read it again, but this time, keep in mind the name Christopher Columbus.

Was the passage easier to read the second time, and is the message now clear? For most people, the answer is yes—but why?

The first time most readers read this verse, they cannot read *from meaning* because key information is missing. Unable to ground the reading act in knowledge already stored in memory, readers are forced to read *for meaning*—or, with the hope that identifying each and every word will eventually cause the verse to make sense. Yet, without the addition of "Christopher Columbus," this seldom happens. Adding Columbus's name serves as a beacon for the brain, pointing the way to the place where knowledge about the explorer and his voyages is stored. The moment reading becomes grounded in stored knowledge, readers are able to *anticipate* or *predict* all subsequent meaning of the passage because they can connect knowledge of Columbus and his voyages quickly and efficiently with the message the author is attempting to convey.

Comprehension is an important concept in reading. After all, the whole purpose of reading is to come away from the experience knowing what the author said. The essence of what we call "comprehension" is establishing a predictive relationship between what *a reader* already knows (knowledge stored in memory) and what *an author* is attempting to communicate. That is why the always efficient brain reads from meaning. In this view, comprehension—or the construction of meaning—*is* the reading strategy used by every excellent reader, making excellent reading an integrated, cohesive, unified process every time it is performed. Comprehension, therefore, is not a separate skill that can be taught. It is the inevitable result when the brain reads right.

Reading from Meaning: Lessons from China

The original Chinese system of writing evolved from picture-based *pictographs* to representative *ideograms*, or symbols designed to directly represent ideas. Figure 2.1 is an example of a written message using ideograms. These symbols represent the idea "The bear is in the water," or, because of the way the Chinese language is structured, more accurately, "The water has in it a bear." Can you locate the symbol for "bear"? Hint: look for the bear's claws. (See symbol no. 6.) Can you find the symbol for "in"? Hint: look for something that is at least partially inside of a rectangle. (See symbol no. 3.) Finally, can you identify the symbol for "water"? Rather than think of water as waves, think of water as a force pushing against another force—land. (See symbol no. 2.)

Figure 2.1   Written Message Using Ideograms

1   2   3   4   5   6

Translation by Debbie Yuan

Although directly meaningful, the ideographic system of writing is cumbersome because of the thousands of individual characters that have to be memorized. Ironically, though, learning the vast number of symbols virtually guarantees excellence in reading because pictures, rather than phonetic representations, automatically focus the brain on meaning. With ideograms, the brain's attention cannot be diverted from meaning as it can with alphabetic systems. Consider this comparison:

In Chinese
- Step 1: Symbol (ideogram)
- Step 2: Meaning

In English (conventional view of reading)
- Step 1: Symbol (alphabetic letter).
- Step 2: Connect a letter or letters to a sound of speech.
- Step 3: Blend the sounds of speech.
- Step 4: Identify the word.
- Step 5: Repeat all of the steps for all of the words in a sentence.
- Step 6: Add up all of the words to derive the meaning of a sentence.

Regardless of whether the written system is alphabetic or ideographic, the purpose of passage reading is the same:

understand the author's message. In alphabetic systems, it is possible to divert the brain's attention away from meaning to a laborious process of figuring out the words. This creates a challenge. If the reader doesn't minimize reliance on the alphabetic system and maximize the use of information already stored in the brain, the quest to construct meaning will be impeded. Excellent readers start *with* meaning to create *more* meaning.

In ideographic systems, it is not possible to divert the brain's attention away from the right cognitive act (the creation of meaning) because the symbols themselves communicate meaning directly. This was an invaluable insight for me in 1994 when the industry giant Motorola contracted with my company to bring the READ RIGHT® methodology to two of its plants in Beijing and Tianjin, China. We were asked to assist employees in acquiring English language skills. Though we had never worked with immigrants who had a meaning-based ideographic system of printed language, I assumed that, because the written Chinese language is meaning-based, none of our students in China would have reading problems.

As we planned time and resources for the projects, I announced to the READ RIGHT program staff my assumption that we wouldn't encounter reading problems. They were highly skeptical. We already had implemented numerous reading-improvement and English-acquisition projects at plant sites for a variety of corporations throughout the United States, and we had never found a single site where there were no reading problems. My staff wondered why it should be any different for the projects in China.

What they didn't initially understand, however, was the significance of learning to read in a meaning-based symbol system like Chinese. I was confident that, if the new view of reading accurately reflected what brains must do to read with excellence, then people who initially learned to read in a predominantly ideographic system *could not* have reading problems in their native language. Their brains could lack knowledge of some symbols, but they simply had to understand on an implicit level that passage reading requires a direct link between knowledge already stored in memory and the meaning conveyed by the author. I predicted that, when applying their reading abilities to an alphabetic system, the majority of Chinese readers would maintain this core understanding about the fundamental nature of the reading process, and they would read in English without any impediment *as long as we did not alter how they intuitively read.* This meant that we would have to keep them focused on meaning and, in accordance with READ RIGHT methodology, completely avoid any strategies related to phonetic decoding or fixation on individual words.

As it turned out, my hypothesis was tested with more than 650 Chinese workers in five cities when we ended up working with employees of Procter & Gamble at three sites in China in addition to the two Motorola projects.

Throughout the five and a half years that we were involved in the projects, we did not encounter one Chinese worker with a reading problem—*not one.* They did as I had expected: they transferred their excellent reading abilities to the English alphabetic system because their basic concept of what they were trying to achieve did not change. We did not redirect their focus to decoding or fixation on every individual word, and consequently, they figured out how to read in English by appropriately *anticipating the meaning* authors were attempting to convey.

We Read Through Our Eyes, Not Our Ears

In the decoding or speech and language view of reading, all readers must associate each letter in a written word with the corresponding sounds of the spoken word, and then blend the sounds together so the word can be identified through "recoding" it to speech. Then readers must decode and recode the same word again and again until a replica of the word is finally encoded into a proposed "word form area" of the brain. Once the replica is stored in the "word form area," it is ready for instant retrieval anytime a reader encounters it on the printed page.

In the *new view*, excellent readers do not use the alphabet for the purpose of decoding, recoding, or matching words to replicas stored in the brain.

Activity: Scrambled Letters

The following paragraph, which circulated all over the world via the Internet in 2004, helps to demonstrate the flawed nature of the decoding view and helps to clarify how excellent readers actually use the alphabet.

> *Aoccdrnig to rseerach, it deosn't mttaer in waht oredr the ltteers in a wrod are prseetend. The olny iprmoatnt tihng is taht frist and lsat ltteres are at the rghit pclae. The rset can be a toatl mses and you can sitll raed it wouthit a porbelm.*

In the paragraph, not one of the words longer than three letters matches any word in the English language. If excellent readers read by decoding, recoding, or matching every word on a page to replicas stored in a "word form area" of the brain, how could readers possibly read this paragraph with any ease and efficiency? They couldn't. And yet, *you* did. How?

Excellent readers use only as much alphabetic information as they need—and no more—to quickly and efficiently establish a link between ideas in their minds and the message an author is attempting to communicate. The brain's search for the most useful alphabetic information comes through an implicit process of *strategic sampling* through which the brain quickly and efficiently seeks and finds alphabetic clues that support predictions about what the author is attempting to communicate.

Scientific studies of excellent readers and their eye movements support this view. Decoding-oriented reading and individual word reading demand strict left-to-right visual scanning. However, vision scientists consistently have found that excellent readers do not use their eyes in this way. Instead, their eyes appear to "sample" text, using a seemingly erratic but strategic pattern of movement. Excellent readers move their eyes several words ahead and then fall back several places behind, apparently seeking whatever is needed at any given moment to help anticipate the text's meaning. Additionally, vision researchers have found that, on average, experienced readers fixate on only 60 to 65 percent of the words in a paragraph. Even new readers, surprisingly, fixate on only 80 percent of the words.

Why would excellent readers scan forward and fall back and fail to fixate on every individual word during the process of passage reading? They do so because it is not necessary to fixate on individual words if a more efficient means of reading exists. Because the human brain is designed to operate efficiently, it will use any and all information available to anticipate what it is that an author has attempted to communicate. It will simultaneously use accumulated knowledge of the topic, knowledge of how language operates, the style of the author's writing, alphabetic information, and more in order to anticipate the text's message.

"Ah," you may think, "but I 'see' every letter and read every word on a page when I read."

Are you certain? Studies have shown that excellent readers routinely make word substitutions when they read, substituting a similar word that is more familiar to the reader for a different word used by the author. They also omit words that the subconscious brain regards as unnecessary and even insert words, as long as the text continues to make sense. Excellent readers tend to be certain that they read exactly the same words the author wrote—but in fact, they don't.

Activity: Excellent Readers Change the Text

The following example comes from listening to excellent readers reading out loud. The text says:

> *People were warned of the high fire danger and urged to be extra cautious.*

An excellent reader reads:

> *The people were warned of the fire danger and urged to be extremely careful.*

Did the two sentences seem the same to you? Without looking back, how many differences did you notice? Now look at the two sentences again. How easy is it to identify the *four* wording changes?

Additional research from vision science supports the idea of strategic visual sampling in efficient reading and also helps to explain why the brain can make sense of the scrambled paragraph that you read earlier. Vision scientists wanted to know where our eyes come to rest while reading longer words—those of five to eleven letters. If excellent reading were oriented to decoding, the eyes logically would fixate initially on the first letter of individual words and then scan in sequence from left to right. However, what vision scientists found is that the eyes come to rest just left of the center of longer words—at the third or fifth letter, depending on the length of the word. Fixating on a word near the center allows the brain to gather a wider array of alphabetic information all at once. This better supports the brain in its search for whatever alphabetic information it needs to keep predictions about meaning coming, or to confirm or reject predictions once they are made.

In the new view, the alphabetic information our brains need in the process of anticipation at any given moment may come from the center of the word, the end of the word, or the

beginning of the word. Or, the brain may choose not to fixate on certain words at all if it can accurately anticipate a
passage's meaning without doing so. Through a process of
sampling the letters on the page and integrating that information with knowledge stored as memory, the brain uses
whatever alphabetic information is helpful at the exact
moment it is needed in the process of making predictions
about text. It efficiently ignores all the rest.

The Predictive Strategy at Work During the Act of Reading

Anticipating text—or the act of predicting an author's message—is used all the time by excellent readers without their
even realizing it. The following activity helps make the point.

Activity: Using the Predictive Strategy

Read the following sentence:

The little boy lives in a _____ .

Most excellent readers, rather than saying to themselves, "The
little boy lives in a *blank*," will naturally and without conscious thought predict the intended meaning. They put a word
in the blank that represents the prediction: "The little boy
lives in a *shoe*" (if this were a nursery rhyme), "The little boy
lives in a *house*," or, for those who live in London, "The little
boy lives in a *flat*." Excellent readers will anticipate, or predict, a logical association grounded in their own knowledge
of locations where little boys live and automatically insert a
word that represents the predicted meaning to complete the
sentence.

Add just one letter, and the brain may modify its
prediction:

The little boy lives in a h___ .

Now *flat* or *shoe* no longer works. The reader settles on, "The little boy lives in a house." As long as the sentence continues to make sense in the context of subsequent sentences, the reader may move on without considering more alphabetic clues. However, a reader who is uncertain about the prediction will choose to integrate more alphabetic information to reduce the uncertainty:

The little boy lives in a h__t.

As the brain integrates this additional alphabetic information, it must reject the previously anticipated meaning and make a new prediction about the author's intended message. Grounding the prediction in knowledge of human dwellings, the excellent reader will now probably predict that the sentence reads, "The little boy lives in a hut." No other predictions readily make sense. Subsequent sentences will confirm the prediction:

The little boy lives in a hut. His home is in a small village in Africa.

Activity: Key Letters

This activity provides another glimpse at how the brain uses select alphabetic information to predict the meaning of printed language. Do your best to read this sentence, even though many letters are missing:

Th__ __itt__ns __r__ s__ft.

This sentence can be read even with one-third of the alphabetic information removed. A high percentage of English sentences start with the word *The*. As soon as the brain has accumulated enough knowledge of how English works, it will know this and easily predict "the" and then move quickly to answer the question, The *what*? The brain will then seek to make additional predictions. Is the author's message about mittens or kittens? Or, the brain may implicitly direct the eyes to look ahead in an attempt to gain more information to assist in predicting the topic. Skipping right over the letter *r*, the eyes may sample alphabetic information in the last word to try to produce a prediction that will unlock the meaning of the entire sentence. From the structure of the sentence and knowledge of mittens and kittens, the brain knows that the last word is most probably *soft*. The phrases *The mittens are soft* and *The kittens are soft* make perfect sense. Information from the sentence that follows the first will help the reader affirm a prediction.

Let's add a second sentence with partial letters and see what happens:

Th__ __itt__ns __r__ s__ft. ____y __av__ w____sk__rs.

Even though half of the alphabetic information is missing from the second sentence, key letters in the last word enable most excellent readers to confirm or reject the accuracy of predictions about the first sentence. The brain can feel reasonably sure that the two sentences are about kittens because kittens have whiskers.

Does the excellent reader *ever* use a pure decoding strategy? Yes, but only when encountering a vocabulary word that is new. When this happens, it is not a reading issue; it is a language issue, and an excellent reader may choose a decoding strategy as an assist in attempting to figure out the meaning of the unknown vocabulary word.

Consider, for example, this term: *bilabial plosives*. If you've never seen or heard the term before, you might attempt to sound it out to see whether any part of it matches a known vocabulary word or word part. If you can't figure out the meaning by associating it with language you already know, you are most likely to either grab a dictionary or simply move on, depending upon how important the term is to your understanding of an author's message or how determined you are to know the meaning. If you do consult a dictionary, you will discover that *bilabial* means "two lips" and *plosives* is a category of speech sound. The sounds represented by the English *b* and *p* are bilabial plosives: air is blocked by compressing the two lips (bilabial). But the airflow, once it is built up, "explodes" (plosives), pushing the lips apart and creating the sound.

Decoding: A Barrier to Reading Development

Old ideas about reading would have us believe that decoding—or the identification of words through a process of sounding them out—is a necessary and normal part of reading development. In the new view, we rarely use a decoding strategy and do so only if we need to provide ourselves with a lesson in new vocabulary. Teaching children to focus on decoding as the main event of reading can be the *cause* of significant reading problems if children do not experiment and figure out for themselves other complex, implicit strategies required for excellent reading. In other words, struggling readers usually become struggling readers because their brains have done *exactly* what they were told to do. Telling a child, "Sound out the word, Jimmy" or "You got that word wrong, Jenny" directs the brain to focus on the identification of words.

A recent encounter with a parent of a determined decoder reinforced the premise that struggling readers often have an erroneous idea of what reading is all about. The mother of a boy in one of our school-based READ RIGHT intervention programs came to the classroom to investigate why her son was saying that he was "not really in a reading class." Her anger turned to confusion when she saw every student deeply engaged with books.

With some probing, this is what I learned: her son didn't believe he was in a "real" reading class because he wasn't working with work sheets and receiving additional instruction in individual word identification strategies, which had been his experience in other reading programs. In the READ RIGHT intervention program, he was being asked to do something radically different. The "something radically different" is the difference between old ideas about reading and the new view.

The activities in this chapter have provided a glimpse of the complex nature of the act of reading. In Chapter 3, we will explore how brains learn and what brains must do to learn to read with excellence.

Success Story: From Struggling Reader to Class Valedictorian

This story wonderfully demonstrates how excellent reading ability can shape a child's future. Matt Hoss was raised by caring and loving parents who are themselves educated and devoted to Matt's schooling. His father is an attorney, and his mother is a secondary school teacher. Yet, in the third grade, when Matt was just nine years old, he scored in the fifteenth percentile on a reading test administered by his school. Such a low level of performance is a clear indicator of a significant reading problem. Through the years, Matt's father shared his son's story through letters written to me. Here is one example:

June 30, 1995

Dear Dr. Tadlock:

Your firm recently assisted my wife, Martha, and me with our son's very serious reading problem. I am writing to express our great appreciation for your help and our great respect for the READ RIGHT program. Our nine-year-old son, Matt, had a significant reading problem, and the best efforts of Martha, his teacher, and me were unable to help. For nearly three years we assumed that hard work and long hours of practice would solve his reading problem. We were wrong.

There is no way I can adequately describe the frustration we experienced when listening to Matt try and read aloud. We have always known he is a smart kid, and he was certainly trying very hard. We spent some time reading with him every day, often an hour or more. The frustration was so great that I even got angry with him more than once because I just didn't think he was trying hard enough. Why couldn't he figure this out?

Martha has a master's degree and teaches math and science at the same school Matt attends. She kept in very regular contact with Matt's teachers, seeking advice and special attention for his reading problem. Matt has always had exceptionally good teachers, and each tried hard to help.

Matt solved his reading problem after twenty-one sessions with READ RIGHT over a two-and-a-half-month period. He has become an excellent and exuberant reader, and he is as proud of himself as we are of him. On his own he is reading three or four books a week now and is reading aloud to his mother, his sister, or me every spare minute.

READ RIGHT helped solve for Matt in two and a half months what the best teachers and programs at his public school and what Martha's and my best efforts could not.

Based on my personal experience with the READ RIGHT program, I know it works. My family is grateful for your expert help.

Sincerely,

Richard T. Hoss

What did we do to help Matt eliminate his reading problem when he was in third grade? We coached him through

continued

relearning the reading process from top to bottom. Rather than use decoding strategies or focus on individual word identification, we helped him implicitly figure out how to access multiple forms of knowledge stored in his brain to anticipate the author's message, and how to use an appropriate concept of excellent reading ability to help him improve his performance.

A few years after we tutored him, Matt was scoring in the ninety-ninth percentile not only in reading but also in every other area of the school district's assessment tests. He continued to excel throughout his school career, becoming the covaledictorian of his graduating high school class of 330 students and being accepted into the prestigious Harvey Mudd College, an elite private school in California. "I love the bookstores at colleges," Matt recently said. "I spend hours in bookstores just because they have such interesting theories and scientific ideas." Not bad for a young man who at age nine had a significant reading problem. Matt's life is forever changed because, rather than focusing on individual words, he now reads to produce reading that makes sense, feels comfortable, and seems just like conversational speech.

3

The Marvelous Brain and How We Learn to Perform with Excellence

As a girl, I would often hear my mother say, "If a thing is worth doing, it is worth doing well." Perhaps she knew intuitively that excellent performance at anything is not a random event. Rather, excellence must be intentionally constructed by an individual's brain, deep below the level of consciousness, and encoded as a part of the neural circuitry.

This has important implications for reading. It means that most reading problems result not from structural brain differences, but from differences in how excellent readers and poor readers have "learned" to read—or, more specifically, differences in the information encoded in the neural circuitry constructed to guide the reading process. The quality of the operation of the neural network—whether it is faulty or efficient—depends wholly on how the individual reader *subconsciously* constructed the complex neural network in the first place.

The idea that the quality of the neural circuitry determines how well a child reads offers both good news and bad news for those who desire to help young children become excellent readers.

- **The bad news:** it is possible for well-meaning and loving people in a child's life to unintentionally provide guidance or an environment that directly contributes to a reading problem.
- **The good news:** nearly every child can be coached into building a neural network to guide reading that operates correctly, producing excellent reading ability. Such coaching can be provided purposefully if the excellent readers in children's lives know how to do it.

For you to become an effective coach, it is essential that you have a basic understanding of how brains learn any process and how every brain learns to perform with excellence. This knowledge will help you make good decisions as you encounter unexpected situations and will help you understand why you are doing what you are doing as you coach your child to excellence in reading.

How the Brain Operates—Simplified

For most people, just the idea of brain science is intimidating. There is a reason we joke about not being brain surgeons. The volume of knowledge required to develop expertise in the field can be overwhelming. Yet, the basics of brain function really aren't that hard to grasp, and knowing how the brain functions is vital to understanding how every excellent reader quickly and efficiently reads newspapers, magazines, poetry, and books. Gaining this understanding becomes much easier if you think of the brain as being somewhat (but not entirely) like a living computer, rather than a mass of gray matter.

What is it that computers do? They are designed specifically for the storage, retrieval, and use of information. A tremendous amount of storage is available on our computers for us to save everything from our literary masterpieces to our day-to-day business transactions. Once stored, this information is ready and waiting for our quick and efficient retrieval. However, before computers can perform these functions, someone had to program them to do everything necessary to operate efficiently and effectively.

The human brain has an even greater capacity for information storage and retrieval and is much more adaptable than a computer. Computers are fixed in how they operate and primarily use one program at a time, storing information to a series of microchips or a disk drive. The human brain, on the other hand, is capable of changing itself and performing multiple processes simultaneously, encoding related information through chemical and electrical systems that leave imprints in various regions of the brain. This encoding occurs through the interactions of neurons, which work together to form neural networks or neural circuitry.

Programming the Brain: The Role of Neural Networks

Computers are hardwired, meaning that they cannot change how they are programmed. The brain, however, is wonderfully *soft-wired*. It can change its own "wiring," which involves what are called *signal pathways* connecting one neuron to another. The brain can disconnect, reconnect, and construct countless signal pathways as it seeks to be ever more functional and efficient. To give you an idea of the sheer volume of this constructive activity, in a one-eighth-inch cube of gray matter in an adult brain, there are approximately 300,000 neurons, 39,360 feet of "wiring," and 300 million connections (or synapses). When children are born, they have most of the neurons, but they have very little of the wiring! (See figures 3.1 and 3.2.)

Programmers hardwire computers, but who soft-wires the human brain? We do! Every infant, child, and adult begins the lifelong process of soft-wiring from the moment human brain development begins. Babies who kick in the womb are figuring out how to move their legs, perhaps in part to reposition themselves in the confined space. Toddlers have to teach themselves to walk by figuring out balance, coordination, and muscle movement. Children and teens who are fascinated with skateboarding don't go to "skateboard school." Instead, they teach themselves how to *ollie* (jump a board upward) and *grind* (ride the skateboard on a curb or rail). No outside force soft-wired their brains for the balance, coordination, and movement required to be successful—they simply figured out the wiring on their own.

Thus it is with all human learning related to the performance of processes, also known as *procedural learning*. In the absence of a physical defect, the level and quality with which we perform thousands of functions depend on the effectiveness of our own soft-wiring. In addition to the procedural, or "how to," knowledge that each of us encodes in our neural networks, our "soft-wiring" also includes all the factual information we know and the beliefs and opinions we hold.

Figure 3.1   Neural Networks in Infants at Three Months Old

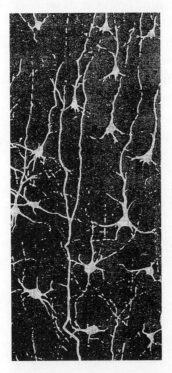

Our "wiring" begins before we are even born. As the artist's rendering indicates, by three months of age, children have already "sprouted" a significant number of connections among the neurons in their brains. The encoding of everything we learn occurs through the interactions made possible by the neural circuitry we build.
Medical Art Services/Photo Researchers, Inc.

Figure 3.2 Neural Networks in Toddlers at Two Years Old

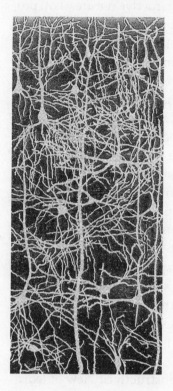

By two years of age, children are much more knowledgeable and functional than they were at three months, and the neural circuitry in the brain reflects the increased complexity of the child's world. *Medical Art Services/Photo Researchers, Inc.*

When we turn on a computer, we have conscious, or explicit, knowledge about how to operate the machine. What the computer actually does to operate, however, lies deep within its network of circuits and memory chips. We are aware of the result of the computer's operation, but most of us aren't aware of what it had to do to get the result.

Our brains are like that, too. We have some explicit knowledge about how to do things such as talk, walk, or ride a bicycle, but the mechanisms that actually enable us to do these things reside deep within our brains, operating *implicitly*. We are not aware of the neural networks that we construct and then access to perform functions, but they are there, nonetheless, guiding every aspect of our physical and cognitive abilities. Our soft-wiring does not occur consciously.

Jean Piaget was one of the world's foremost authorities on how young children learn to perform processes. He provides this example of the subconscious interactive nature of all procedural learning: ". . . [a baby] tries to grasp a hanging object but only hits it without getting his hand around it. What results is interesting to the infant, and he tries to make it happen again by means of reproductive assimilation involving a series of regulations and corrections that continues until the ability to perform the act becomes stable."

Technically speaking, the "reproductive assimilation" described by Piaget translates to the signals sent between neurons—or the "neural firing patterns"—repeated over and over again by the baby's brain. The "series of regulations and corrections" refers to continuous modifications in the baby's soft-wiring made as he seeks to figure out how to be successful. In the process, the baby constructs the neural circuitry he will use throughout life to guide the grasping process. Figuring out grasping involves *interaction* with some aspect of the baby's environment and *construction* by the baby of the neural circuitry required to guide the process, giving rise to Piaget's well-known *interactive constructivist* view of learning and cognitive development.

According to the interactive constructivist view of learning, to soft-wire our brains to guide any process, we must do the following:

1. Come to understand exactly what we are trying to achieve (the goal).
2. Anticipate or predict what we must do to achieve the established goal.
3. Make a first attempt based on the initial prediction.
4. Implicitly analyze the result of the attempt.
5. Judge whether the attempt was successful.
6. If unsuccessful, implicitly predict what modifications might lead to success.
7. Make a new attempt.
8. Continue to use this cyclical, implicit process until we figure out how to succeed at achieving the goal.

Over time, as we move through this predictive cycle, we construct the neural network that eventually guides the process we seek to perform. All skills we learn and all knowledge we acquire involve this type of soft-wiring, or encoding of information and construction of neural circuitry. The encoding of information in the brain is the essence of learning.

In Figure 3.3, a photograph of neural circuitry from a cultured sample shows what encoded information looks like in the brain. The brain can change its encoding at will—this is called plasticity. The plasticity of the brain means the brain constantly changes itself—assimilating new information and making additional connections within the junglelike mass of circuitry.

Although we are aware of all the declarative knowledge that we construct in our brains—facts, beliefs, and opinions—we are not aware of *procedural* knowledge because it operates implicitly, and thank goodness for that! Imagine how slow

Figure 3.3   Neural Networks Magnified

Imagine 300,000 neurons and 39,360 feet of "wiring" in a one-eighth-inch cube of your gray matter! The complexity ensures efficiency and flexibility as the brain gathers what it needs to make sense of whatever it encounters. *Q-L Ying & A. Smith Wellcome Photo Library*

and inefficient we would be if, every time we wanted to walk across a room, we had to think through every aspect of the process!

- Step 1: Maintain balance.
- Step 2: Signal muscles to contract and lift foot.
- Step 3: Maintain balance.
- Step 4: Lift foot.
- Step 5: Maintain balance.
- Step 6: Signal muscles to contract and bend the knee; and so on.

Instead, the human brain implicitly accesses neural networks constructed specifically for walking, and these neural networks automatically, without conscious thought on our part, integrate useful knowledge and learned patterns of movement as needed.

Programming the Brain: The Role of Executive Functions

What is it that makes it possible for our brains to coordinate, integrate, and control multiple neural networks as they implicitly plan what is required to perform complex functions or construct networks for the guidance of new processes? *Executive function* performs this all-important task. For example, a baby constructs the neural network to guide the process of sitting up. The mastery of the movements and balance required for this process becomes procedural knowledge, or process knowledge, stored in the brain. Later, as the baby attempts to figure out how to stand, the brain implicitly seeks any procedural knowledge that may help in determining the complex, integrated process of standing. The knowledge about movement and balance that has been stored for the process of sitting up may be accessed and applied as the baby attempts to figure out the process of standing. In this way, neural networks that the baby has already constructed help with the construction of new neural networks for other processes.

Such integration and coordination have been described as a "symphony" in the brain, with neuronal executive functioning acting as the conductor and neural networks serving as the many musicians. The integration and coordination of neural networks becomes a crescendo of electrical and chemical activity throughout the brain. The crescendo almost instantaneously yields functions we choose to perform—functions such as walking, talking, dancing, or any of the other thousands of processes we have learned—including reading.

Our brains can handle needed variations in the performance of functions only because we can access and integrate information stored from past experiences. For example, a toddler just learning to walk trips over a toy the first time he encounters one in the middle of the floor. After several spills over different toys, he figures out what is causing the falls and determines that it is more efficient to step over or go around the objects in his path than to continue falling. This becomes new information stored in the brain, and as the toddler implicitly locates and integrates this information when needed, he ceases to fall over his toys. Eventually, the toddler is stepping over or walking around objects automatically because his brain knows this is what it has to do to avoid falls. The child doesn't consciously think about it anymore. He just does it.

In 2003, neuroscientists S. B. Laughlin and T. J. Sejnowski observed: "The more we learn about the structure and function of brains, the more we come to appreciate the great precision of their construction and the high efficiency of their operations. Neurons, circuits, and neural codes are designed to conserve space, materials, time, and energy." The brain, therefore, is designed for efficiency. As long as it is not provided with inappropriate information and misled by an erroneous goal, the brain will figure out for itself the most efficient means for solving a problem and give up on strategies that do not work.

Programming the Brain for Excellence

How well a speaker speaks, a drummer drums, or a skater skates depends on the quality of the neural circuitry constructed to guide the respective activities and on the efficiency of executive functioning. Most people can speak, but very few do so with the power and richness of poet Maya Angelou. Her deep voice, meaningful emphasis on just the right words and phrases to convey the intended meaning, and careful enunciation are highly developed—and guided by neural circuitry constructed specifically to produce excellence in the area of poetic recitation.

Most people can tap sticks on a tabletop, but few can drum with the talent and skill of Buddy Rich. His meticulous control of muscle movements enabled him to turn what otherwise might have been considered taps and bangs into pleasurable rhythmic music. How was he able to deliver such a refined sound? He did it by constructing neural circuitry designed specifically for excellence in the use of drumsticks and drums.

Many people can skate, but there is only one Michelle Kwan. Kwan has worked hard to become one of the greatest figure skaters of all time. How did she do it? You guessed it— by constructing neural circuitry designed specifically to produce excellence in the area of figure skating.

Angelou, Rich, and Kwan each achieved excellence through hard work, determination, and, literally, the creation of neural circuitry constructed specifically for world-class performance. Each became a master of performance through the same means—by figuring out the complex processes independently. Every person who achieves excellence ultimately does so because he or she settled for nothing less. We alone construct the neural circuitry and perfect the neural functioning that results in our performance.

Our human brains are a marvel of memory and physiological communication, instantaneously integrating ever-expanding knowledge from wherever it is stored. Only through the construction of neural circuitry specifically designed for efficient and effective integration and coordination of information can *any* function be performed well. (See figure 3.4.)

Contrary to Popular Belief, We All Learn in the Same Way

A widely accepted assumption in education circles is that individuals learn in different ways, and that a mismatch between

Figure 3.4 Neural Activity Occurs in Multiple Regions of the Brain During Passage Reading

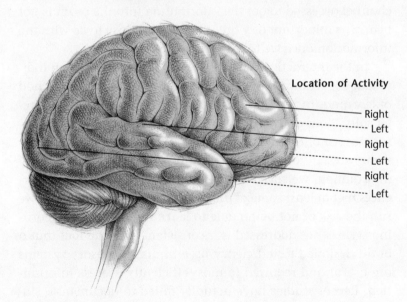

Location of Activity

Right
Left
Right
Left
Right
Left

Brain studies during sentence reading have found activity in both sides of the brain and in front, middle, and back regions, implying that passage reading is complex and requires integration of neural activity in multiple brain regions.
Brain drawing by Kate Sweeney Medical Illustrations

an individual student's learning style and instruction (including a teacher's "teaching style") explains why some otherwise bright and capable children struggle with classroom learning. The basic styles of learning are considered to be through listening (auditory), seeing (visual), and touching (kinesthetic). The assumption is that an auditory learner may struggle if the learning activities are heavily dependent on visual processing, the visual learner may struggle in a hands-on learning environment, and so on.

All of us, of course, access information from the environment in the same way—through the sensory channels of vision, hearing, touch, taste, and smell. And we all have the potential to watch a Neil Simon play and learn nothing about playwriting, listen intently to Mozart and learn nothing about how to reproduce classical music on a piano, and use a sewing machine in an effort to make a dress and learn little about dressmaking. The point is this: the particular sensory channel accessed to get the information into the brain is not nearly as important as what our brains choose to *do* with the information once we take it in.

In the interactive constructivist view of learning, an individual's learning style is not the person's dominant method of learning. Instead, it is a preference. For example, if I prefer salty foods and you prefer sweets, we both respond to sensory information—but each has a different preference. In the same way, if you prefer visual input and I prefer auditory information, we each may be happier if we have our preferences met at least some of the time. However, the idea that we run the risk of not being able to learn if our preferred learning style is not addressed is inconsistent with the fact that a brain designed for efficiency uses whatever sensory systems are useful and required to most efficiently process information. Recent studies have actually failed to document a significant role for a specific learning style in learning.

In the interactive constructivist view, brains learn to perform processes in fundamentally the same way—by predicting how a process is done, making attempts, analyzing the attempts, making adjustments, and continuing the cycle until success at a task is achieved. From person to person, brains construct neural networks to guide processes in the same experimental, interactive way.

The idea that every brain performs its primary function—*learning*—in fundamentally the same way should not be surprising. The same is true of all the other organs of the body and their primary functions (with the exception of individuals who are born with defective organs). Everyone's heart pumps blood in fundamentally the same way, everyone's lungs take in oxygen in fundamentally the same way, everyone's digestive system processes food in fundamentally the same way (whether that food is salty or sweet!), and everyone's brain—that marvelous organ for making sense of the world—constructs neural circuitry, or learns, in fundamentally the same way. Wouldn't it be somewhat of a freak of nature if all our organs worked in fundamentally the same way *except* the brain?

Performing a Process with Ease and Efficiency

Savants are individuals who develop an uncanny skill for performing a specific function exceptionally well. Individuals with mild to severe brain dysfunction occasionally turn up as savants. An explanation from an interactive constructivist point of view is that these individuals' brains become fascinated with a specific function or skill and choose to remain focused on the performance of that skill until they figure out how to do it with remarkable ease.

In a way, young children who teach themselves to read are savants. They have taught themselves to perform reading with remarkable ease and efficiency, and the ability stays with them throughout life. It stays with them for only one reason: the brain is performing the process of passage reading *correctly*. The brain no longer needs to make implicit modifications to the neural network guiding the process because the network already produces the desired end result, which is excellent reading.

There is much we can learn from these little reading savants and all other individuals who teach themselves to perform a process with ease and efficiency. Every single one achieves excellence in the same way. They all construct neural circuitry that is specifically designed to perform the process well. It really is that simple. Like all learners, they have encoded information into the brain in the form of a neural network that they activate every time they want to perform the process. But what made it possible for them to construct this kind of efficiently operating neural circuitry?

There are three requirements for constructing neural circuitry designed specifically to produce excellence:

1. Developing a concept of what constitutes excellence in the performance of the process
2. Maintaining strong intent to achieve excellence
3. Employing a repetitive, implicit cycle of anticipating—or predicting—what must be done to achieve success

A concept of excellence, strong intent, and the use of a predictive strategy to figure out how to perform with excellence are tools used by top athletes and artists all the time. Equipped with strong intent, they establish a standard of excellence (e.g., in tennis, "serve an ace"; in golf, "land the ball in the middle of the fairway"), and they do not give up until they have achieved the defined standard. How do they do it? They use a predictive strategy to make subtle, implicit modifications that cause them to perform the task differently each time they attempt it, until they ultimately achieve success. As their brains figure out how to serve the ace or land the ball in the middle of the fairway, they encode the information into their brains by *remodeling* existing neural circuitry or constructing a new neural network to guide future performance of the task. This is how all humans learn to perform a process excellently.

In formula form, it looks like this:

Model for Constructing Excellent Performance

Develop a Concept + Maintain + Use a Repetitive = **Become**
of Excellence   Strong Intent   Predictive Strategy   **Excellent**
                                                            at Performing
                                                            a Process

Excellent readers use the same three requirements to figure out how to read with excellence. In formula form, the process looks something like this:

Model for Constructing Excellent Reading Ability

Develop a Concept + Maintain + Use a Repetitive = **Become an**
of Excellent   Strong Intent   Predictive Strategy   **Excellent**
Reading   to Achieve   to Figure Out How   **Reader**
                      Excellent   to Make Excellent
                      Reading   Reading Happen

Remember the characteristics in Chapter 1 that researcher
Dolores Durkin discovered when she studied young children
who figured out the reading process for themselves? She found
that these children shared the following traits:

1. Had parents who read to them often, an activity that
   helped them develop an appropriate concept of excellence
   in reading
2. Were determined to figure out the reading process for
   themselves
3. Requested that the same books be read to them again and
   again, increasing the predictability of text
4. Asked many questions and made many requests as they
   spent time with books, including alphabet books

The only way to figure out any process is to experiment on an
implicit level. We can safely assume, therefore, that these children were using a predictive strategy to conduct their own
implicit experiments as they sought to figure out for themselves how to make reading happen. Their numerous questions
and requests had a subconscious purpose—to get the job done.

What Durkin's early readers must have done to figure out the reading process for themselves is reflected in the formula for becoming an excellent reader.

In Part II, Chapters 4 through 6 provide suggestions and instruction for ensuring that your child develops a correct concept of excellent reading, maintains strong intent to become an excellent reader, and has the opportunity in an appropriate environment to use a repetitive, predictive strategy to figure out the complex implicit process. Read these chapters carefully and begin immediately to use the activities with your child. Once you have had an opportunity to practice these foundational techniques with your child, read Chapter 7 and begin the purposeful effort of guiding your child into reading with excellence.

Remember, as you read these chapters and then engage in each of the activities, you will begin the process of constructing your own neural network to guide interactions with your child. To learn how to coach your child effectively, you will need to gain a clear understanding of each technique, attempt to implement it, assess your performance, make adjustments, attempt again, and continue the cycle until you can coach with excellence. All of us really do learn in fundamentally the same way!

Success Story: A Young Man with Down Syndrome

The following is an amazing story of the power of the new view to cause the brain to completely remodel the neural circuitry that guides the performance of a process.

Jordan Null has Down syndrome and a long history of participation in special education and after-school remedial programs. When Jordan was three, he began to attend developmental preschools and later repeated kindergarten. Between second and sixth grades, Jordan participated in pullout programs for reading and math, including continuous and intensive training forty minutes a day, five days a week, with a reading program considered tops in the field for tapping into multiple senses (vision, hearing, and touch) in the process of learning. By the end of sixth grade, Jordan struggled to read upper-first-grade/lower-second-grade materials. By eleventh grade, Jordan's reading level was assessed in the same late-first-grade/early-second-grade range, and he had a significant problem with stuttering.

Jordan's mother, Paula, heard about READ RIGHT® through a classmate of her son's and decided that she wanted the program for her son, too. Prior to enrollment, Jordan resisted almost all recreational and functional reading activities. READ RIGHT tutors employed by the school performed a program assessment and started Jordan in first-grade-level books. During the year, Jordan's tutors noticed a slow but progressive decline in his stuttering in oral reading activities and significant improvement in his ability to read materials efficiently.

Two years after beginning the READ RIGHT program, Jordan was reading recreationally at the fourth- and fifth-grade levels and was continuing the program with fifth- and sixth-grade reading materials. Though little more was done for him outside the basic READ RIGHT program, in October 2003, Jordan's tutor provided the following report:

> [With Jordan] there is a speech problem, too, and we're seeing progress in areas other than his reading. His vocabulary is growing and so is his ability to communicate with others. He is able to give longer answers to his family. He's not giving up so easily when he is trying to communicate. For example, he was reading a story on whales to his mother, and she couldn't understand him when he said the word "whales." Jordan explained what was happening in the story, and then his mother understood that he was talking about whales. Jordan is also learning how to relate things in his environment to things in stories. He is learning to link vocabulary and concepts in books to his world. This has tremendous benefit for him because it is helping him to read, but it's also helping him to learn about

continued

things in his world. Because he can see and apply things that he is reading about—computers, Christopher Columbus, space, the ocean—Jordan is now more interested in seeking out things that are fact-based and science-based.

Later on, Jordan's tutor reported to us that even though he had not received remedial instruction in handwriting in the last two years, Jordan had made significant improvements in his penmanship as well as in his reading.

Jordan's experience is an impressive story of success. There is a reason that his handwriting and speech skills improved, too. Jordan's brain is learning to *anticipate* and *experiment* in the process of figuring out the complex process of passage reading. Along the way, his brain on an implicit level is figuring out how to use *anticipation* and *experimentation* with other complex processes that the brain guides—processes such as handwriting and speech. Before READ RIGHT, Jordan's brain did not consistently use anticipation and experimentation to produce improved performance. Now he is beginning to more consistently use these all-important brain functions.

PART II

Guiding Children to Become Excellent Readers

Remember the blind men from the East Indian folktale in the Introduction? The sightless men were unable to understand what an elephant is because each one considered only a part of the massive animal. To construct a more accurate idea of what an elephant is, they needed to integrate their diverse observations. Reading is like that, too. For truly excellent reading ability to develop, young readers must access and integrate all relevant knowledge stored in their brains in order to give life and meaning to whatever it is an author is attempting to communicate. They must simultaneously figure out how to access relevant knowledge stored in memory as well as how to plan, control, and coordinate the integration of that knowledge in a manner that causes printed messages to make sense.

Reading is a mosaic of subconscious activity in the brain that is dependent on foundational concepts, such as books tell stories; books make sense; there is a right side up and an upside down to books; you turn pages from right to left at just the appropriate time, not left to right; and books involve warm, fuzzy feelings. The foundation for figuring out the reading process, therefore, can begin before a child is one year old! You don't need to know exactly when a child's brain is "old enough" or ready to perform each part of the process. The only thing you have to do is create an environment in which your child has the opportunity to engage in the activities presented in Chapters 4 through 7. Your child will show you whether or not he or she is ready to participate. In other words, there are no set ages for when the techniques in the following chapters apply. You need to experiment and follow your child's lead, whether at age one, two, three, or older. Never assume that your child is too young to engage in the techniques. Give them a try— and back off if you get no response.

The techniques for working with your child are intended to be flexible and interactive. They are not designed to be applied sequentially, step-by-step. They can't be, because children have to be in charge of their own process of figuring out reading. Develop an understanding of what the techniques are trying to accomplish, and then, as you interact with your child, pay attention to how your child reacts to the techniques and follow that lead.

4

The First Prerequisite: A Concept of Excellence

Walt Disney understood and appreciated the power of human imagination. It was his idea to build the first Magic Kingdom, where the places and characters from storybooks would seemingly come to life. Mr. Disney's first Magic Kingdom did not begin with the wood, plastic, steel, concrete, and computers used to make the theme parks a delightful, interactive experience. The first one—and every one thereafter—began as an idea in Mr. Disney's mind, an idea intended to cause people of all ages to make a connection with childhood stories and fantasies. Ideas are what come to life at Disneyland. If guests like the ideas that are on parade there, they usually enjoy the experience.

Reading and Mr. Disney's Magic Kingdoms are similar in that both are *events* that require a great deal of planning and coordination for the illusions to be effective and pleasurable. Disney's Magic Kingdoms are the destination of choice for millions of people annually because the level of performance is so high that guests experience a near flawless land of fantasy. From the realistic facades to the theatrical "casts" of employees, every detail is orchestrated to deliver a high standard of excellence. Guests know only the end product: Disneyland as a fantasyland providing a few hours of undisrupted entertainment.

Excellent readers, too, have settled for no less than the production of excellence. They know that the act must always make sense, feel comfortable, and seem like conversational speech. Excellent readers are not aware of what they do to cause reading to be a seamless event in their minds. If the myriad activities that occur to make excellent reading happen were above the level of consciousness, it would be like visiting a Disneyland where one could readily see every wire, scaffold, metal bar, foam structure, and costumeless character that, in truth, is under the surface of the Disney experience. In an environment where the mechanics are totally exposed, it would be difficult for any visitor to Disneyland to tune out all of the unwanted information in favor of experiencing an undisrupted fantasy.

In the same way, awareness of all the mechanics performed by the brain in the process of efficient and effective reading would be difficult to tune out if they were exposed. Therefore, for reading to be completely seamless, it is necessary for the underlying process to remain invisible while the conscious brain focuses on what an author intends to communicate.

The Definition of Excellent Reading

What, then, is excellent reading? And, if it occurs below the level of consciousness, how can a reader know when it is happening? Let's look a little more closely at the three important characteristics:

1. **Excellent reading makes sense.** Excellent readers focus on the meaning (or message) an author is attempting to convey, not on the mechanics of the reading process. They virtually always understand what they are reading. If

they do not, they recognize that it is because they lack key information.

2. **Excellent reading feels comfortable.** Excellent readers experience the process as effortless. Rather than focus on any perceived mechanics of the reading process, their minds are busy reconstructing the author's message almost as though the author were reading the story or explaining a concept to them.

3. **Excellent reading, when done out loud, sounds natural to the listener.** When excellent readers read out loud, they read in a manner that accurately conveys the ideas and voice the author intended to convey. Oral reading ends up sounding as natural and smooth as it would if it were a conversation.

When children, on a subconscious level, understand that all three of these things must be present for reading to be excellent, they will have created for themselves an appropriate yardstick by which they can judge their own attempts at reading. How old must your child be to create and use this yardstick? It depends largely on language development and when she forms the internal intent to figure out the reading process (both of which vary widely among children). Once that yardstick has been personally established, your child will have an important tool for holding her brain accountable for figuring out the complex process of excellent reading.

A child who doesn't figure out what constitutes excellent reading ability on a subconscious level will have no yardstick and may settle for less than excellence. In settling for less, the child unknowingly enables the brain to perform the process incorrectly. This is the critical line that separates an excellent reader from one who struggles. In the process of reading development, a child destined to become an excellent reader will settle for no less than the production of comfortable reading that makes clear and perfect sense. In doing so, children gradually construct neural circuitry designed specifically for the production of excellent reading ability.

Techniques to Help Your Child Develop a Concept of Excellent Reading

Your child can develop the all-important yardstick—or standard of excellence for reading. Quite wonderfully, children probably begin to craft this ability through nonreading activities. The following fun and meaningful techniques will assist you in helping your child develop an appropriate concept of excellence for reading and other functions.

Technique 1: Encourage a Habit for Excellent Performance

Your home is your child's first and most important "classroom." The environment you create for your son or daughter there is essential to helping the child establish an appropriate concept of excellence for reading—and for the performance of any other task. However, rather than beginning with a process as complex as reading, let's start with an activity in which your child's ability to achieve excellence can be easily and immediately observed. The following example focuses on setting the table, a highly explicit nonreading activity. What you learn from this example can be easily transferred to many other situations as you work with your child to encourage a habit of pursuing excellence. Establishing a pattern for the expectation of excellence in your home will be helpful as your child seeks to master other activities and processes, such as cleaning a bedroom or folding laundry.

Establishing the Concept of Excellence for Setting the Table. Children need to see excellent performance modeled for them. Begin this activity by making it a habit to set your table the same way every time you dine. In this example, I am using a table setting that is common in American homes: one plate placed neatly in front of each chair where a family member will sit, a fork placed neatly to the left of the plate, the knife placed to the right of the plate (cutting edge turned toward the plate), and the spoon placed neatly to the right of the knife. However you do it in your home, be sure to do it the same way for every formal mealtime.

Get out the plates, knives, forks, and spoons and encourage your child—in this example, a daughter—to set the table exactly the way you've been setting it.

If she places the plates haphazardly and a knife, fork, and spoon together in a jumble by each plate, say: "Thank you for helping me set the table. Do you think it would look nicer if the plates were like this?"

Rather than describe how the plates should be placed neatly in front of each chair, show your child how a plate should be positioned. For the moment, don't worry about the silverware. Give your child the chance to develop a concept of excellence for the placement of plates.

If your child says it doesn't look nicer, don't disagree with her, and don't go any further. She doesn't want the lesson— but she did hear the message that she didn't do an excellent job with the plates. It was an important lesson delivered in a friendly environment. The next time she goes to set the table, she may surprise you and comply.

If your child says it does look nicer and makes a decision to fix all of the plates, then silently evaluate whether or not she truly did it well.

If she didn't do well, say: "Those look much better. I see one of your plates that is placed just like mine. Can you find it?" If she can't, show her. Your point is to continue to call attention to what excellent plate placement really looks like. Don't be concerned with having all of the plates perfect. You've made your point.

Once she is placing most of the plates correctly, change your feedback.

Say: "I see a plate that isn't placed correctly. Can you find it?" If your child can't find it, point it out to her and briefly explain why it wasn't well placed.

Over time, your child will see to it that all of the plates are placed correctly. When she does, say: "Wow, look at that! That looks so nice. You did such a good job of placing the plates in just the right spot!"

The most important features of this kind of interaction are:

- You provided the child with a positive environment to figure out how to place plates correctly.
- You provided the child with an accurate concept of what it is to place plates correctly by sometimes calling attention to aspects of the job that were genuinely well done and other times calling attention to aspects of the job that were not well done. The feedback was immediate, accurate, and friendly. Notice that blanket praise ("Wow, look at that!") is withheld until excellence at the entire task is fully achieved.

You can provide appropriate encouragement to your child by making a big deal out of aspects of the job that were truly done well. For example:

- If she sets only one plate correctly, say: "You did such a nice job with that plate. Why don't you choose who gets to sit there tonight?"
- Or, if she sets all of the plates correctly, when other family members or guests come to the table, say: "Look at what a nice job our daughter did at placing all of the plates. She did it all by herself."

Notice how the focus remains on achieving the established standard of excellence. It is imperative that your feedback be honest and authentic.

- If she doesn't place any of the plates correctly, say: "Thank you for putting the plates on the table. Would you mind straightening them up so that they look like this?"

- Then show her how to do it again. If she doesn't want to do it, don't force the point. You want to keep the event a positive experience so that your child will be willing to make an attempt at another time.

When you feel your child is ready, ask her if she wants to learn where the silverware goes.

- If she says no, then she's not ready to learn more. It is important that you don't force the activity. If she develops negative emotions around table setting (or any other activity to which you may apply these techniques), she may abandon the learning process! Let her tell you when she is ready—but, in the meantime, keep offering her the opportunity to help you set the table.
- If she indicates that she does want to learn where the silverware goes, you'll need to make a decision. Do you want to show her how to place the knife, fork, and spoon all at the same time, or do you want to focus on just one or two of the utensils?

Either way, make the activity fun and meaningful by making up a story about the placement of the utensils. For example:

- Say: "The fork is Mommy, and Mommy is going to stay on this side of the plate because she's busy fixing dinner in the kitchen." As a physical demonstration to your child, place the fork exactly as it should be placed to the left of the plate.
- Then say: "Now, while Mommy is fixing dinner, you and Daddy (or Grandpa, another relative, or a friend) go for a walk to the other side of the plate." Again, as a physical demonstration, have fun "walking" the knife and spoon together to the right side of the plate. As you do, say: "Now, which one is Daddy—the knife or the spoon?"
- When she chooses one, say: "OK, Daddy goes here." Place the knife or the spoon, whichever one the child chooses, exactly where it should go on the right side of the plate.

- Then say: "Which one is you?" Place the remaining utensil exactly where it should go.
- Then say: "Do you think you can place the knives, forks, and spoons where they go beside all of the plates?"

If your child says yes, then let her try. If she says no, then say: "Do you want me to help you?"

Follow your child's lead. If she says she doesn't want to do it, don't force it. Wait for another day. If she asks you for help, show her what to do and, as you do, revisit the story of "Mommy, Daddy, and You" to help your child remember the placement. Above all, keep the activity *fun!*

In this activity, the most important features of the interaction are:

- Your child has been provided with a friendly environment in which to figure out how to place plates and silverware correctly.
- You held your child to the established standard in a positive way.
- You allowed her to interact with the activity by creating a meaningful way for her to remember where the knife, fork, and spoon needed to be placed to achieve the standard of excellence.

Once your child knows what an excellently set table looks like, you might, without looking at the table that she has just set, ask her in a casual and friendly manner if she did an excellent job or a so-so job. Then, after she is no longer in your presence, see if you agree with your child's judgment. If you do, there is no need to do anything. If you do not agree, call her to the table.

- Say: "You said this was a so-so job, and I'm trying to figure out why you think that. It looks excellent to me."
- Or: "You said this was an excellent job, but I disagree. Can you see why I disagree?"

If she can't, give her feedback about why, in your judgment, the setting was not done excellently. The purpose is to make sure your child knows if she is performing excellently or not. Your child needs to be in charge of her own progress. Relying on you to tell her if she has performed excellently undermines her learning. She must *know* if she is performing excellently or if she is not.

Applying Excellence to Any Activity. In a similar manner, it is possible to establish an appropriate standard of excellence for nearly any activity—from folding laundry to cleaning bedrooms to a more sophisticated activity such as tying shoes. For other nonreading activities, be creative, and above all, remember the key features for helping your child develop an appropriate concept of excellence:

- Demonstrating excellent performance
- Encouraging her to hold herself to the established standard
- Checking in to make sure she knows when she is performing excellently and when she is not
- Giving her the opportunity to interact with the activity in a friendly and meaningful environment

Technique 2: Honestly Appraise Your Own Reading Ability

As we saw in the table-setting activity, modeling genuine excellence is key to helping a child learn to establish an appropriate concept of what it is to perform with excellence at any task. Consequently, for the future success of your child's reading development, you need to know whether or not you truly are an excellent reader so that you can be sure to provide appropriate models of excellent reading for your child. This requires a little honest self-evaluation.

If you can read out loud without the slightest hesitation, producing reading that sounds just like conversational speech, then you are an excellent reader. If you display a pattern of pausing, sounding unnatural in any other way, using decoding or sounding-out strategies, not appearing totally comfortable as you read, or reading slowly and otherwise inefficiently, you likely have some degree of a reading problem—whether it is minor or severe. If any of these issues emerge as you read, find books that appear to you to be easier to read. For example, if you have a lot of trouble reading aloud *Charlotte's Web*, by E. B. White (HarperTrophy, 1974), then stick to simpler books with more pictures and less print on each page. More on this will be addressed later in this chapter.

Admitting the presence of even a slight reading problem can be a tough pill to swallow, but it is a necessary one. The kind of reading you display—as your child's model for what is and is not excellent reading—has the potential to influence the concept of excellence that your developing reader forms on a subconscious level, and, as has been discussed, establishing an absolute standard of excellence in reading is essential for proper reading development.

Technique 3: Be Authentic and Honest About Your Child's Performance at Any Task

Now that you've been honest about your own reading ability, it's time to consider how it is possible for you to create learning barriers for your child if you aren't willing to be honest about your child's performance. My dad provides a great example.

When I was sixteen, Dad taught me how to drive. I was certain I was on the right track because every day, when we finished with that day's driving lesson, he told me what a great job I'd done. I decided I was ready to get my license, so I made an appointment to take the tests. I passed the written exam on the first try—and bombed the actual driving test. After I failed, the truth came out. My parents had secretly admitted to each other that they hoped I would fail because both recognized that I would be a menace on the road! I thought I knew how to drive and was properly prepared to pass the test because of my father's seemingly sincere feedback. In truth, I wasn't just a bad driver; I was dangerous! In an effort to encourage me in learning to drive, my dad had provided me with erroneous information that completely undermined my implicit understanding of what excellent driving was. He didn't intend to do this, but he did it all the same.

Your communicating on an implicit level (through a process of modeling excellence) that reading needs to make sense, feel comfortable, and sound like conversational speech will help your child develop a true concept of excellent reading from the start. She will be less likely to become satisfied with halting, error-ridden reading. And when she first starts reading, you will give her honest feedback about her initial attempts. Remember: false praise undermines an appropriate concept of excellence.

Technique 4: Model Excellence in Reading

It has been understood for years that children who are raised in homes where they are read to frequently have a better chance of becoming excellent readers. Experts do not yet fully recognize why. Many assume that the practice instills in children a concept of reading or a love of reading. There is, however, at least one other significant reason for reading to your child—to *model reading excellence*, thereby helping your child to subconsciously understand what it is she is trying to achieve.

Obviously, books are what we commonly read aloud to our children. Any type of book that captures your child's interest is appropriate. Other activities involving reading materials from daily life work just as well, such as:

- Reading cereal boxes and simple instructions to your child
- Writing notes to your child and reading them to her
- Making it a daily event to read the newspaper comics together

- Being the scribe as your child creates messages for birthday, get-well, and thank-you cards (Be sure to read what
  you transcribe back to her.)

Whatever and whenever you are reading, seek items of
interest to your child. For example, if there is an item in a
magazine or newspaper or on the Internet about a character
or animal your child enjoys (cats, dogs, pandas, Donald Duck,
and so on), read a paragraph or two aloud and engage your
child in a conversation about the material.

- Say: "That was interesting. I learned something new from
  that."
- Or: "I thought that was interesting. What did you think?"
- Or: "I didn't know that the name for pandas in China
  means 'giant bear cat.' Did you?"

Any opportunity to read to your child is an opportunity
to model excellent reading ability. As you read, focus on what
the author is communicating (the meaning) so you produce
oral reading that makes sense, feels comfortable, and sounds
natural.

Technique 5: Evaluate "Errors" Using the New View of Reading

In the old view of reading, inserting a word in the text, omit-
ting a word altogether, or substituting one word for another
would usually be considered an error because developing
readers are expected to identify every word on the page.

In the new view as presented in this book, an excellent
reader does not identify words; the reader constructs ideas and
meaning from text. It is perfectly OK if the reader chooses different language to construct the author's message—*as long as
the reader doesn't significantly change the meaning.* In the old
view of reading, any change to text indicates a *weakness in
reading.* In the interactive constructivist view, word substitutions, insertions, and omissions in the process of passage

reading are signs of *strength in reading* because they indicate that the reader is focused on figuring out the meaning rather than figuring out the words. Excellent readers don't even notice the changes in the language they make during the process of reading.

Examples of Appropriate Text Changes. The sentence says: "The little boy bounced the ball." The reader reads:

- "The small boy bounced the ball." This still sounds natural, makes sense, and doesn't change the author's intended message.
- Or: "The boy bounced his ball." The language is still natural, and the author's intended message has not been changed.
- Or: "The small child bounced the ball." The author's intended message is not significantly changed.

Examples of Inappropriate Text Changes. If any reader changes the text in such a way that the sentence no longer makes sense, sounds awkward, or doesn't reflect the meaning intended by the author, that's not OK. These are inappropriate changes to the text and are errors. Excellent readers do not make errors; they make logical, acceptable changes. Inappropriate changes occur only with readers who have built erroneously operating neural networks for reading. Here are some examples of inappropriate text changes.

The sentence says: "The little boy bounced the ball." The reader reads:

- "The little boy bounced the bell." This doesn't make sense.
- Or: "The little boy bounced ball." The language isn't natural.
- Or: "The little girl threw the ball." The author's intended message is significantly changed.

Identifying Errors. If you make any errors while reading to your child, casually announce what you did wrong, read it again, and, when you read correctly, acknowledge that the error has been fixed. The following examples will help you.

- When the text doesn't make sense, say: "That didn't make sense. Let me read it again." After you fix the error, say: "Ah, that made sense."
- When the language doesn't sound natural, say: "That didn't work. I'll read it again." After you fix the error, say: "That sounded much better, didn't it?"
- When the author's message is significantly changed, say: "I changed the meaning. I'll read it again." After you fix the error, say: "OK. That's what the author meant."
- When your reading is awkward and didn't feel comfortable, say: "That didn't feel comfortable. Let me read it again." After you fix the error, say: "That felt so much better."

Statements like these communicate implicitly to your child that reading needs to make sense and feel comfortable and that, to the listener, the language needs to sound natural.

Above all else, remember this about opportunities to model excellence in reading to your child: *your goal* is to show your child that passage reading is a pleasurable experience characterized by reading that makes sense, feels comfortable, and sounds like conversational speech. Accomplish this and your child will develop an implicit and appropriate concept of what it is to read with excellence.

Techniques to Use if You Are Not an Excellent Reader

Children growing up in homes where literacy skills are marginal or poor are more likely to struggle with the "concept of excellence," in part because their role models (adults and siblings) seldom read aloud or, when they do, they read poorly. Their reading sounds unnatural because they are focusing on individual word identification as the main event of reading. Why? They were told to do so in their own early reading experiences. This misunderstanding about the nature of the reading act (figuring out words rather than figuring out meaning) contributed directly to their reading problems. They are likely to communicate this erroneous thinking to their children, and this can easily set a child on the wrong path to figuring out the passage reading process.

If you are not an excellent reader, use these tips to ensure that your child receives appropriate models of excellent reading. Parents or siblings who are excellent readers can also use these techniques.

Technique 1: When Reading Aloud, Make Sure the Reading Sounds Like Conversational Speech

Look for books that you don't have to struggle to read out loud. Again, if you cannot efficiently and effectively read a book like *Charlotte's Web* aloud, look for some of the many delightful shorter children's books with more pictures, shorter sentences, and simpler language. Visit your local library or bookstores and spend a few minutes reading aloud from the vast number of books available. Continue to look for "just the right book" that is both of interest to your child and relatively easy for you to read. When you get the book home, practice reading it silently until you can read it comfortably and naturally to your child. If you do this consistently and hold yourself accountable to a strict standard of excellent reading, your brain is likely to remodel its erroneously operating network, thereby improving your own reading ability!

Another technique is to create your own reading materials by writing notes and then reading them to your child. Don't worry about spelling or about reading the note just as you wrote it. Instead, think about what the note says, and read the message in a manner that sounds just as if you are engaged in a conversation.

Technique 2: Provide Your Child with Other Models of Excellent Reading

Provide children with other models of excellent reading by exposing them to excellent readers. You do not need to be the model of excellent reading ability for your child, but you do need to be the one to see that she has models of excellence.

You can ask a family member, friend, or neighbor who is an excellent reader to read to your child regularly. Later on, as your child starts to read, you can help by recognizing whether or not the reading is truly excellent and providing appropriate feedback. You do not have to be an excellent reader yourself to judge whether your child is reading with excellence.

Another way to expose children to excellent reading is by checking out children's audiobooks from your local library. Make it a joint activity by holding your child on your lap with the book. Both of you can listen to the book being read on tape as you read along silently, and you can help your child turn the pages at the right time. After the two of you do this together a few times with the same book, you may be able to read it to your child naturally and comfortably.

You can also ask an excellent reader to tape-record a few short children's books for your child. If you don't know any excellent readers, be bold enough to ask your local children's librarian to put a few short stories from your child's collection on tape. Provide the blank tapes and tape-recording equipment for the library, if necessary. The worst thing the librarian can do is say no.

Also at your local library, attend story times for children regularly. After each story time, talk with your child about the story's message and characters (to implicitly communicate that reading involves a message that makes sense). During your talk, comment on how natural the reading was ("It felt just as if the reader was talking to me") and how comfortably the reader read. Don't overdo it—your comments need to be authentic and not contrived. In any way you can, place a value on excellent reading ability.

Things to Avoid When Communicating Excellence

In the process of communicating the concept of excellence to your child, here are the two most important things to avoid:

- A false sense that the child has performed a task with excellence when, in truth, the performance had flaws
- Any focus on figuring out each and every word as the main event of passage reading

In addition, *never* do the following:

- Ask your child to perform a task without first modeling an appropriate standard of excellence.
- Make a blanket statement to your child that he or she has done a task well when the child hasn't met the established standard of excellence.
- Forget to acknowledge when performance (or aspects of it) has met the established standard of excellence.
- Create a situation in which the child relies on your judgment to determine whether or not her attempts are excellent. Children need to learn to judge their own excellence.

When your child begins to make attempts at reading, *never* say or do anything to cause her to focus on individual words, such as pointing at words while you read or saying any of the following:

- "What's that word?"
- "Sound it out."
- "Let me help you with that word!"
- "Good for you! You got that word!"
- "Look more carefully at that word."
- "That's not what that word is."
- "You read that word wrong."

All of these statements—or anything similar—give your child the message that reading is about identifying words, rather than constructing a passage's meaning.

Finally, avoid overdramatizing stories. Doing so for fun is OK occasionally, but it should not be the norm because it conveys to children that dramatic theatrical reading is the goal and hence the standard for excellence. A developing reader needs to know that excellent reading ability is not dramatic. Instead, it sounds like conversational speech—as though the author of a book were in the child's own mind. The developing reader needs to know that, to the listener, reading sounds natural.

Please know that while you may not understand every aspect of the suggestions presented in this book, *they work!* Do your best to comprehend the purpose of the techniques, and follow your child's lead in choosing which to use and when. Feel free to attempt to apply the concepts in ways other than those suggested. If you do, keep in mind that reading at all times needs to make sense, feel comfortable, and seem like conversational speech, and readers always need to focus on the meaning an author is conveying and *not* on individual words. Stick to the basics and your child will likely do just fine.

Success Story: A Little Girl Who Has the Right Idea

A business associate who is the father of a charming five-year-old recently shared with me an experience from his daughter's kindergarten class. He has been using the techniques outlined throughout these pages.

To his pleasure, his daughter is in the early stages of figuring out the reading process, to the point that she can read the text in some books in which the language is very repetitive and, therefore, highly predictable. She is one of the few early readers in her kindergarten class.

In her classroom, the little girl's teacher is doing exactly what all kindergarten teachers should do—she is reading to the children on a regular basis. On one particular day, however, the teacher chose to read a story in—an—unnatural—and—slow— pattern,—accentuating—each—and—every—word. We can only assume that she was attempting to send her students a message—that reading requires a focus on individual words.

What do you think our little early reader did? She raised her hand and pointed out to her teacher that she was reading incorrectly. "You're supposed to read so that it sounds natural, just the way you talk," she told her teacher. Good girl!

5

The Second Prerequisite: Strong Intent

Have you ever known someone who overcame incredible odds to be successful—perhaps someone with a physical disability or mental challenge? Who would have thought that a child in leg braces until age eleven—a victim of scarlet fever and pneumonia—would become one of the fastest and most celebrated women runners of the twentieth century? That's exactly what happened with Wilma Rudolph, the first American woman to win three gold medals in an Olympic Games. She participated in her first Olympics at age sixteen and became known as the "World's Fastest Woman" by age twenty, when she won her gold medals and set Olympic and world records in the 200- and 400-meter dashes.

A life-threatening health problem should have ended the career of world-class cyclist Lance Armstrong, but it didn't. In 1996 at age twenty-five, at what should have been the height of his physical health, Armstrong was diagnosed with a form of cancer that had already spread to his lungs and brain. His hope for survival, let alone of ever again attaining world-class athletic status, was in serious jeopardy and rested in complicated surgeries to remove the cancerous tumors. However, just two years later in 1998, Armstrong was winning races again, and by 1999, he led an American team to its first victory in the Tour de France. He is now a six-time winner of the world's most prominent bicycle road race.

A colleague of mine is a huge fan of Temple Grandin, a world-renowned scientist in the field of animal management who also happens to be autistic. Traditionally, autistics have been shut out of careers in academic settings, largely because of difficulties communicating, but not Grandin. She is demonstrating to the world that it is possible for autistics to direct their minds in highly productive, creative, and insightful ways.

Have you heard of the Jamaican Bobsled Team? When this tropical team first turned up on the slopes in Europe, the world couldn't help but laugh. Jamaica has neither Alpine mountains nor snow. Yet, this team of men was determined to compete on an Olympic level with individuals from countries where snow is a natural part of the landscape. To compete, these athletes had to figure out for themselves what it was that produced excellent performance associated with bobsledding and then experiment over and over on slopes in the United States with the same heart and soul as their counterparts. The world stopped laughing and began admiring the team when the members eventually performed well enough to earn the respect of their peers.

All of these people provide examples of what is possibly the most powerful aspect of the human mind: *intent*. Words synonymous with *intent* include *purpose, resolve, determination, earnestness, eagerness,* and even *meaningfulness*. One of my favorite scientists and authors, Jeffrey M. Schwartz, M.D., calls intent *mental force* and credits Roger Sperry with first defining it as "electrochemical traffic" between neurons in the brain, reminding us that intent is actually a biological process.

Intent: A Force of Nature

Evidence from neuroscience supports the reality that humans can develop most of the skills and abilities to which they set their minds, so long as they can generate *mental force*. In his book *The Mind and the Brain*, Schwartz notes that most victims of brain injury can regain a measure of lost functions if their physical systems are still operational and the patients can focus their attention. Schwartz calls mental force a powerful "force of nature."

Rudolph, Armstrong, Grandin, and the Jamaican Bobsled Team all used this powerful force to overcome barriers that had the potential to undermine their success. Where did their determination come from? Odds are it had something to do with how they grew up—whether it was influence from the people who loved them or an event or series of events that caused them to know that they could choose to shape their own futures.

Whatever it was, something caused each of these highly successful individuals to develop unwavering intent to overcome the barriers they faced and become excellent at a desired task or function. As a result, on a subconscious level, they did not cease to experiment until they successfully performed with excellence. They directed full attention and focused mental force on the challenges at hand, and in the process, they caused physical changes to their brains. They literally changed their own neural circuitry so that excellence would be produced. Intent truly is a powerful force of nature!

Intent shapes what we learn. The brain is intent on satisfying its wonderment and curiosity with everything that captures its interest and attention. Think of the little boy who, at the tender age of two, can pronounce the names of a dozen dinosaurs! He can do this because his brain is fascinated with prehistoric reptiles, and as a result, he absorbs dinosaur names like a sponge. Why should a two-year-old be capable of pronouncing complicated dinosaur names when many adults struggle to remember them? Simple: the two-year-old possesses strong intent to know the dinosaur names, and the adult does not.

Intent equips us to build our own knowledge because it powers the mental force required to encode information through the construction of neural networks. For learning related to processes, either we generate and maintain the implicit intent needed to perform to a particular standard of excellence or we do not. Individuals who experience success hold on to their intent as though it were the family fortune. People for whom success at a task is elusive have, at a sub-conscious level, wavered in their intent.

Before we go further, know that intent and motivation are not one and the same. Intent occurs primarily implicitly through biological processes below the level of consciousness. Motivation, on the other hand, is a more surface-level, explicit event. Children can be motivated to clean their rooms by the promise of a gold star or a cookie at the end of the task, but the external motivation has no bearing on the type of job they do in the process. Individual intent controls how well they ultimately perform. They can possess intent to get the job done as quickly as possible to receive their reward, or they can possess intent to do the job with excellence because that is their concept of a clean room. See the difference? Motivation may influence our decision to begin a task, but intent is the biological mechanism that we all use to get the job done.

Intent: A Powerful Force in Reading Development

Children who form strong intent to read with excellence will desire to learn for the joy, excitement, and other rewards inherent in reading. Such intent will cause them to be persistent as they strive to figure out the complex process of passage reading. You can help your child form the strong intent required for reading development, but you must do so intentionally, and you are more likely to succeed if you know how.

For decades, parents have accomplished this for the most part in an unintentional, haphazard manner, without even knowing or recognizing how they did it. Consider, for example, families in which one child teaches himself to read and another doesn't. For the son who teaches himself to read, the parents' role may have been as simple as expressing joy at his early interest in reading and making sure that he had plenty of access to books. As for the daughter who doesn't teach herself to read, her parents may have expected her to have an early interest, forced books on her, and then expressed disappointment when they found she wasn't interested. Pressure and disappointment both have the potential to undermine intent.

Children who possess insufficient intent are easily discouraged and frequently give up. When this happens, they abandon any effort to improve their performance. All too often, such children settle on grossly inaccurate explanations of why they haven't yet been able to figure out reading—explanations that have the potential to undermine their performance in all aspects of formal schooling. They become consumed by self-defeating statements such as, "I can't do this. I'm too stupid. There must be something wrong with me."

As your child's first and most important coach, you can help shape his ability to use mental force—or intent—to become an excellent reader. You do it in subtle ways, by helping the child do the following:

- Develop a subconscious desire to perform with excellence
- Build confidence in his ability to experiment and act
- Develop a sense that it is OK to take reasonable risks with reading

All of these qualities will contribute significantly to the intent your child will form to figure out the complex process of passage reading. That intent must be authentic and implicit, residing below the level of consciousness. It cannot be faked to please you, a teacher, or any other well-meaning adult. Intent to succeed at any given task comes from deep within us, as a result of something that fascinates us, that captures our interest, or that we desire. To learn how to read with excellence, we must first form intent, and then our intent must continue to fuel mental force while we construct the necessary knowledge. When intent wavers, we cease to perfect our knowledge or performance. It is that simple.

Techniques for Developing Intent to Become an Excellent Reader

The rest of this chapter is devoted to providing you with techniques for helping your child—in these examples, a son—form strong intent to become an excellent reader. Read and study them closely. As you do, keep in mind that the activities need to be light and relaxed, not mandates for your child. One of the greatest barriers to the formation of intent is anxiety. It is possible to cause children to become anxious about their reading development if they begin to feel that they are not meeting a time schedule that their parents have set. Relax and enjoy the journey—don't force it. As children come to see the value of reading, they will form their own intent.

Technique 1: Influence Your Child to Value Reading

As a parent, you are the most important person in the life of your child. Your child wants to be like you. If you clearly communicate that you value reading, he is likely to value reading, too. And, if he does, then he is more likely to establish strong intent to figure out how it is done. Though externally imposed motivation rarely has a lasting effect on establishing internal intent, the things that we value *do*. The following tips are designed to instill the value of reading in children. They do not constitute a new approach to encouraging reading development in children, but they are vitally important.

Model your own appreciation for reading. Do the obvious. Let your child see you reading often, and show that you enjoy it. This applies to all experienced readers in the household: moms, dads, brothers, sisters, and so on.

Read aloud. Read to your child whenever and wherever possible—while waiting for an appointment in the doctor's or dentist's office, in the car when the family goes on a long trip, before naptime and bedtime, or when snuggling together during a quiet moment at midday. When your child is feeling sad and wants to be comforted, smile and ask if he'd like to read a story. When he needs a distraction to stop worrying about a missing pet or skinned knee, do the same. When you just want to make a personal connection with your child, read to him. As you read together, make sure he can see both the pictures and the text.

Develop a reading routine. Build reading into the structure of the daily routine. Bedtime is a great opportunity to encourage your child to spend fifteen minutes on his own with reading (picture books for a very young child, simple books for a developing reader). You can set the example by spending time yourself with books at bedtime. In this way, your child can be encouraged to see reading as a "grown-up" thing to do.

Choose reading. In the presence of your child, model choosing to read over another activity. Show your child (don't tell him) that reading has tremendous value and is more desirable than other activities. Encourage him by giving him choices, but by "stacking the deck." For example, say: "Do you want to turn out the light and go to sleep, or do you want Mommy to read you a story?" Or: "Do you want to take your nap now, or do you want to hear a story first?" Don't force him to choose reading. Rather, give him the opportunity to choose it. You don't want to create any negative associations with reading, because doing so runs the risk of undermining intent.

Show your child how to access books. Visit bookstores and libraries with your child regularly, and get excited with him about books. Enjoy the process of choosing a book, and be sure to check out or buy one for yourself. Let him pick a book for any absent family member, and let him be the one to present the book.

Choose reading materials that enhance a trip. When you go on trips, take special books along and make time to read them to your child. Choose some books that connect with the nature of your trip. For example, if you're taking a trip to the beach, read a story about a day at the beach. Later, as you do beach activities, make connections with what you read in the book. For example, say: "Let's build a sand castle like the kids in the story we read."

Use reading for a strategic purpose. Use books to give a heads-up about coming events. For example, if Grandma and Grandpa are coming for a visit, read a book about such a visit, and ask: "Who do you think is coming to visit us?" Read a story about a messy room, and say: "Let's go look at your room. What do you think? Is it messy? Do you want to clean it up like the boy in the story? Let's do it together."

Give books as gifts. Give books as gifts to your child and other family members for birthdays and other holidays. Help your child choose a gift for a family member or friend. Guide him in choosing a story the family member or friend may enjoy based on consideration of the person's interests.

Talk about what you are reading. Encourage your child to discuss with you stories you have read to him. Talk about what happened in stories and about the characters. Also, make sure your child has opportunities to hear you talk to others about what you are reading.

Make affirming statements to your child regarding the value you place on reading. Consider these examples:

- "I'm so glad I know how to read. It lets me know about such interesting things."
- "Today I learned about . . . ."—then share details about what you read.
- "Thank you for letting me read to you. I love to read."
- "I wish I had more time to read."
- As you are tucking your child into bed, say something like: "Good night. I'm going to bed early so I can read. Would you like to look at a book in bed for a few minutes, too?"

Technique 2: Communicate the Usefulness of Reading

If your child perceives reading to be useful, he is more likely to establish a strong intent to become an excellent reader. The following tips, if consistently applied, will help instill an intuitive sense that reading is useful.

Share what you learn. In the presence of your child, freely share what you learn from reading. For example, say: "I read the most interesting thing . . . ." Or: "Wow, I read a really interesting article that said . . . ."

Encourage your child to realize the usefulness of print outside the home. While driving or visiting town, share what street and building signs say and then explain why it is useful information. Encourage your child to predict and "read" the signs. Point to a sign and say: "What do you think that sign says?" This will help him begin to predict what particular signs say every time he sees them while you are driving or walking. If you explain the signs correctly, he will come to know that, for example, a stop sign says and means stop, a yield sign says and means yield, the signs on the corner of an intersection are the streets' names, the sign above a store is its name, and so on.

Write and read love notes to your child. If your child is going to spend the night with a grandparent or family friend, write a note to him and ask the person to read it to him before bedtime. Or, during the day, leave a special toy and note with your child's day-care provider. Ask the provider to give him the toy at a special time and then read the note to him. This will help communicate that print has usefulness that extends beyond the covers of books and the walls of your home. It's a nice way to express your love, too!

Help your child dictate and mail a letter or card to someone he loves. Communicate the excitement the recipient will feel when she receives a letter from your son. Let your child pick out the paper or card, the envelope, and a pretty stamp. Say something like: "Grandma will be so happy to receive your letter. She's going to love this pretty stamp, and most of all, she's going to love hearing from you." Have your child dictate the letter to you as you write it down. Then read it back to him. If he asks to add more or wants to make changes, follow his lead. You can modify this activity with birthday cards, get-well cards, and so on. Let your child put the letter in the mailbox. This type of activity teaches children that verbal language can be translated into symbols and that these symbols can be interpreted with great meaning by readers. The activity also shows children that they have something of value to say to others.

Encourage early writing ability. Encourage your child to write letters of his own, even if he does not yet know how to form the letters of the alphabet. Ask him to read the letter to you. When he does, even if every scribble is unrecognizable, say: "I'm so glad you wrote this down so I can keep it and read it again and again. Thank you. When you can read, I'll write letters to you."

Follow instruction-oriented reading materials. Cook with your child and follow recipes, or build a model and follow instructions. While doing so, comment on how glad you are that you can read so that you can try new things. Read each step aloud and then do what the instructions say, thereby showing him that reading has the ability to teach us new things and guide us through activities.

Create lists with your child. Before you start a project, whether it is cooking dinner or building a model, brainstorm with your child a list of what will be needed for the project. Let him see you composing the list. When the list is completed, read it to him and discuss how items on the list will contribute to the project. Refer to the list as you start the project and frequently as you continue and complete it. In this way, you will show your child that reading and writing help us accomplish things that we set out to do.

Technique 3: Help Your Child Feel Excited and Enthusiastic About Reading

If your child is excited and enthusiastic about reading, he will obviously be more likely to generate a strong internal intent to read comfortably and easily on his own. There are a number of ways you can help create excitement and enthusiasm.

Keep a Variety of Books in Your Home. Providing a variety of books from which your child can choose is more likely to capture her interest. For example:

- Children's classics
- Award-winning books
- Books that are wonderfully illustrated
- Wordless picture books in which you can "talk" the story
- Alphabet books
- Picture books that are made predictable by repetitive language
- Picture books with minimal print on each page
- Books with content that is of particular interest to your child

More on the use of different types of books will be discussed in Chapter 7.

Integrate Books and Reading into as Many Family Events as You Can. Fun book-centered and reading-centered activities and events also can help generate enthusiasm and excitement for reading. Try several of these ideas:

- **Make book-buying an anticipated event.** Figure out a way to take your child on much-anticipated shopping trips just to buy a new book. You might establish a routine of visiting a favorite bookstore every payday. This will give him something to look forward to and show him the relationship between earning a living and being able to use money for things that are important to both of you. Or, if your local bookstore discounts books on a particular day of the week, choose that day to go. However you choose to do it, find a way to build book outings into your weekly or monthly routine.

- **Make books part of the planning process for events.** Plan fun outings or even fun activities around the house, and before you engage in them, find a book that relates to the activity. For example, before a shopping trip, read *Eloise's Guide to Life*, by Kay Thompson and Hilary Knight (Simon & Schuster 2000), to your child and enjoy talking about all the fun activities in the book (including shopping!). If it is a special event, the two of you might talk about it beforehand, go to the library a day or two in advance, and look together for a children's book that relates to the event. Enjoy finding and reading the book together and anticipating all the similar things you'll see and do at the event.

Show Your Own Excitement About Books and Reading. Enthusiasm is contagious. If you are enthusiastic about books and reading as you interact with your child, he will be, too.

- **Talk with your child about stories.** Talk with him about the fun, silly, scary, or exciting things that are happening in the story. Ask him lots of questions and give him plenty of time and opportunity to respond. In addition to helping him learn to appreciate stories, this will help him develop thinking and language abilities, too. The *Eloise* books provide a great example. As you read them, draw your child's attention to aspects of the content that you find interesting. For example, after reading that Eloise is a little girl who lives at The Plaza Hotel in New York, say: "Wow! Eloise lives in a fancy hotel! Can you imagine what that would be like? Do you think they have room service? (Explain room service, if necessary.) Or a doorman? (Explain what a doorman does, if necessary.)"
- **Interact with your child about the characters.** It's helpful to set the expectation that characters—whether they be people, animals, aliens, or "others"—are an important part of stories. Children will figure out for themselves that

characters also teach us about life and can become our "friends." Ask: "Who do you like in that story?" Or: "What do you like (or dislike) about those characters?" Make observations about the appearance or behaviors of the characters. (For example: "She has brown hair just like you!" "He likes baseball just like you!" "She says funny things, doesn't she?")

- **Encourage your child to anticipate what will happen next in the story.** Predicting how a story will evolve increases your child's excitement and enthusiasm by engaging her in a very deep way. It also has a special purpose in reading development. It helps your child understand on a subconscious level that reading involves anticipating an author's message and sets the stage for focusing on meaning rather than words. For example, say: "What do you think is going to happen next?" Or: "What do you think is on the next page?" Much more on this is discussed in Chapter 6.

Look for Ways to Help Your Child Become a Member of a Broader Community of Readers. Social connections with others who enjoy and value reading is another way to create excitement and enthusiasm about reading. You can help create those connections through the following:

- **Arrange for your child to enjoy books with playmates.** Children don't have to be able to read to enjoy books. They can show each other pictures and use the pictures to talk about things each likes or dislikes. Books are a great conversation starter, even for young children! Encourage playmates or siblings to "read" to each other by retelling the stories using the pictures as cues.
- **Participate in story hours.** If offered by schools or at the nearest library, story hours can turn reading into an outing and a social occasion.
- **Organize read-aloud opportunities.** If you can, organize an event in your community in which young children are brought in once a month to be read to by older children in

the school. Younger children love to be read to by older children, and older children feel a sense of pride when they can share a personal accomplishment like the ability to read with others. You can also organize read-aloud opportunities with other mothers in your own neighborhood or with friends who have children around the same age as yours.

Subscribe to a Magazine for Your Child or Help Him Join a Book Club. Help your child sign up for an age-appropriate magazine or book club. When the magazine or book arrives in the mail each month, create excitement about the new stories and reading activities you are about to share. For your convenience, we have compiled a list of children's magazines and book clubs along with their website addresses. Please keep in mind that this list is provided for your information only and does not constitute an endorsement. Be sure to make your own thorough inquiry as to costs, obligation, and appropriateness for your child and your family. If you do not have access to the Internet, inquire at your local public or school library. Librarians may be able to offer additional options.

Magazines your child may enjoy include the following:

- *Cricket* magazines for all age levels (*Babybug, Ladybug, Click, Spider, Ask, Cricket, Muse*): cricketmag.com
- *Highlights for Children*: highlights.com
- *Kids Discover*: kidsdiscover.com
- *National Geographic Kids*: nationalgeographic.com
- *Ranger Rick* and others (*Wild Animal Baby* and *Your Big Backyard*): nwf.org
- *Zoobooks*: zoobooks.com

Book clubs your child may enjoy include the following:

- Children's Book-of-the-Month-Club: allbookstores.com/ bookclubs/childrens_book_of_the_month_club
- Dr. Seuss Book Club: edu-central.com/education/scholastic _drseuss.html

- Kids' Book Planet: bookplanetbookclub.com
- Little Wonders Children's Book of the Month Club: cbomc .com
- Stuart Brent Children's Book Club: stuartbrent.com

Technique 4: Set an Expectation That Your Child Will Become an Excellent Reader

Subtle communication to your child that you are confident he will eventually develop a specific ability can have a significant impact on internal intent. He respects and admires you and will seek to rise to your expectations. The statements suggested here will challenge your child's subconscious to figure out reading.

- After reading to your child, occasionally say things like: "Won't it be great when you can read stories on your own? Then you can read to me!"
- While interacting with alphabet books, when appropriate say: "Wow! You know so many of these letters. That will help you be an excellent reader someday." Remember, do so only if your child can actually identify a significant number of letters.
- When buying a book for your child, say: "I can't wait to read this book to you. Someday you'll be able to read it all by yourself. Maybe you will read it to me then, OK?"
- After reading to your child, say: "When you're an excellent reader, will you still let me read books to you?" Or: "Grandma said to tell you that as soon as you know how to read, she wants to be the very first person to hear you read a story."

Things to Avoid When Guiding Your Child to Develop Strong Intent

There are many ways to inadvertently set children on the wrong path to reading. To prevent that from happening, first and foremost, it is important to engage in appropriate behaviors for guiding children to form strong intent to figure out the process. It is also useful to be aware of (but not overly focused on) what can undermine intent. Keep in mind the following suggestions:

- Don't do anything to cause your child to dislike or dread reading, or to feel obligated to figure out the complex process on *your* time schedule. Your goal should be to help him build strong intent to become an excellent reader so he will eagerly direct his "mental force" to the challenge of figuring out all of the implicit and explicit aspects of the reading process on his own, when he is ready.
- Don't use your child's devotion to you as a way to exert control over his choices about reading. Intent is not generated if the child is reading only as a means of pleasing you. It is generated through sincere desire and the sense that reading will be useful and will make life better.
- Never force your child to listen as you read or to spend silent time with reading material. Create opportunities to read together or alone, but always let him decide if he wants to participate.
- Never communicate to your child that reading is "hard." Doing so is a sure way to undermine intent. Remember, brains by design avoid activities that they perceive on a subconscious level as difficult or, worse, impossible. It is important not to set this expectation in a child's subconscious.
- Don't be phony in your interactions with your child. Don't "gush" about reading as if you are trying to "sell" it. Children can see right through such behavior. They might conclude that there must be something wrong with reading or that you are trying to force reading on them. Either way, your child may become resistive.

Success Story: Hope Is an Important Aspect of Intent

A child's intent is often severely impaired when a reading problem develops. It can, however, be restored when the child is provided with real solutions to a reading problem. Here, a mother of a former struggling reader encapsulates how success and hope are rekindled when severe reading problems are authentically and permanently addressed.

> I just want you to know that this whole experience thus far [with READ RIGHT® tutoring] has been the best thing that has ever happened to JayJay. You have given him something that I thought was lost: HOPE. I know that as a mother you can understand how heartbreaking it is to see someone you love so much struggle so hard and still get no results. JayJay and I both know that all of that has changed, and I could never thank you enough for relighting the end of that long dark tunnel he was following.

6

The Third Prerequisite: The Predictive Strategy

By the time children are old enough to be interested in reading, their amazing brains will have already formed neural networks to perform thousands of processes, such as wiggling a finger or toe, smiling, talking, walking, or playing games. Children don't learn how to do any of these activities by breaking them into discrete parts. Rather, they begin to perfect the ability to smile, talk, and walk by first anticipating, or predicting, what internal and external information the brain needed to gather, integrate, and coordinate in order to perform the targeted function—and then giving it a go!

When a child fails at early attempts while learning something new (and children will fail at first because they have to make mistakes in order to figure out any process), the marvelously developing brain will analyze the results by comparing them with the standard of excellence the child has established. The child's brain will predict what modifications are needed to produce the desired result, and then it will make the modifications and try again. All of this takes place below the level of consciousness. So long as there is sufficient intent, the child will continue to use this cycle of prediction—try, fail, predict the modifications needed, try again, and so on—until the function is mastered.

Mastery means the child has figured out exactly how to perform a process according to an established standard of excellence the child has established and has soft-wired the discoveries into his or her brain by constructing a neural network to guide future performance. Children will use this neural network to perform the process with excellence again and again throughout their lifetimes! Mastering functions begins before birth. It is what the brain is designed to do.

Mastering a "Model" Activity

The experience of a young friend of mine who aspires to become a fashion model illustrates how the cycle of prediction works to build neural circuitry for guiding a new function. Sixteen-year-old Kate had a graceful walk, but she discovered that professional models use a different and somewhat unnatural walk on runways. For weeks, Kate struggled to get the right balance, hip motion, and arm movement. The old neural circuitry that Kate constructed years before to guide the process of walking kept taking control of the function, and consequently, she could not produce the unusual walk. She hadn't yet constructed the *new* neural network to guide the *new* walk.

Already equipped with strong intent, Kate initially used observation to help her establish a new concept of excellence for the runway walk. She watched the precise movements of accomplished models: a slight lean back, feet planted flat, hips rotating with slight exaggeration, shoulders down, and arms relaxed. She couldn't do any one of these movements separately and make the walk look right; she had to figure out how to integrate them so they became a cohesive movement.

To be successful, Kate had to establish a standard of excellence for her runway walk so that her brain would know what it was trying to achieve. Then she had to use a *predictive strategy* over and over until her brain implicitly figured out how to make it happen. As she made attempts, judged which were successful and which were not, and then made new attempts, she formed the new "soft wiring" required to guide the more rhythmic walk. Now, whenever necessary, she activates the neural circuitry she constructed for the walk. She no longer needs to think about it; her implicitly operating brain just makes it happen.

Every person who develops exceptional ability in performing a process does so because he or she has constructed the neural circuitry to guide the process in such a way that excellent performance is produced. Remember: excellence is the "goal" or expectation that a brain sets. Expecting to perform with excellence is different from merely expecting to perform a task. Demanding excellence sets an uncompromised high standard of performance, and the standard becomes the yardstick by which the brain measures the success or failure of all attempts. The brain that seeks to figure out a process continuously asks itself key questions:

- "How might I make this happen?" The brain wonders.
- "Maybe like this." The brain experiments again and again.
- "Nope. Oh, I know! Like this! Nope. Wrong again. I'll try this. Nope."

If intent is strong enough, the brain does not cease to use this predictive strategy until it achieves the standard of excellence it has established.

The Predictive Strategy: The Key to Reading Development

The predictive strategy works for passage reading in exactly the same way as it does for all other process-oriented learning. The learner strives to figure out how to achieve reading excellence—reading that is efficient (quick and comfortable) and effective (with full comprehension). With a clear understanding of what constitutes excellent reading and in the presence of sufficient intent, the brain engages in an implicit cycle of prediction to answer the question, What do I have to do to make excellent reading happen?

Children who demonstrate readiness to figure out the passage-reading process by willingly engaging in any kind of reading activity possess enough stored knowledge to understand the messages expressed by authors in many children's books. They know, for example, what a duck is and that ducks like water. They know that a dog has four feet and a tail that wags. They know how families and friends typically work and play together. How did they learn all of this? They learned it by interacting with the environment in which they live and using a predictive strategy to make sense of all that they encounter.

Odds are that when your child was first told that a particular animal was a duck, she (or he) began to make predictions about what constitutes "duckness." When she pointed to a swan and said, "Daddy! A duck!" she received immediate feedback that her prediction about what makes a duck a duck was wrong. "No," you promptly said, "that's a swan." This caused her to formulate another prediction and, at the next opportunity, try again. By engaging in a cycle of prediction aimed at answering the question of what makes a duck a duck, she eventually figured it out and soft-wired the information into the appropriate place in her complex of neural networks, ready to be located and activated whenever needed to make sense of any story about ducks that Mommy or Daddy reads to her.

Any kind of mental activity that involves interaction with the environment requires such prediction or anticipation. Therefore, it should not be surprising that a predictive strategy is fundamental to the process of passage reading. Excellent readers anticipate the meaning expressed by an author, and anticipation is possible only from the perspective of what a reader already knows. You experienced this phenomenon firsthand when you read the verse about Christopher Columbus in Chapter 2. In passage reading, prediction provides the link between what you already know and the author's intended message. This link is the essence of what educators call *reading comprehension*.

Comprehending is what the brain does consistently and effortlessly every moment of the day. In the same way that most hearts come into the world ready to pump blood (you don't have to teach them to do it), most brains come into the world ready to comprehend (you don't have to teach infants to comprehend; their brains simply begin to do it). Parents who worry about an older child's reading comprehension don't have the same concern in other arenas of the child's life. Children with sufficient language ability don't struggle to comprehend TV cartoons or what people say to them—they seem to struggle only to comprehend reading material. Why should this be so?

It happens when, on a subconscious level, children operate on the belief that the main event of reading is to figure out what each and every word is, rather than to read *from meaning*—making an immediate link with knowledge already stored in the reader's mind. When readers struggle with comprehension in reading, it is because they are reading to identify words rather than reading through a process of grounding anticipation of a passage's meaning in knowledge already stored in memory.

The child who reads efficiently (quickly and comfortably) and effectively (with full comprehension) has successfully used the cycle of prediction to construct neural circuitry to guide the passage-reading process with excellence. When activated, the neural network operates on the text, causing the reader to anticipate what the author intends to communicate, thus using a predictive strategy to efficiently and effectively construct the author's intended meaning.

Using the Predictive Strategy to "Figure Out" Reading

Your child has already successfully used the predictive strategy to figure out many, many processes required to function in and make sense of the world around her. If properly encouraged, your child's brain will automatically call on the predictive strategy to figure out the complex, integrated process of passage reading. It will proceed through these steps:

1. Predict how it might achieve excellence in reading
2. Attempt to achieve excellence according to the prediction of how that might be done
3. Fail in its first attempts to achieve excellence
4. Subconsciously assess the result, comparing it with the established standard of excellence
5. Adjust the prediction so excellence is more likely to occur
6. Make another attempt

The predictive cycle is continuously repeated until the brain figures out the reading process. In model form, the predictive strategy looks something like Figure 6.1.

This cycle of predicting, attempting and failing, analyzing the result, adjusting the prediction, and making a new attempt *is* the cyclical predictive strategy. In the process of using a predictive strategy, your child's brain has spontaneous access to all of the knowledge it has accumulated to date, and it calls on relevant knowledge whenever needed as it strives to figure out the process of reading.

It is important for you to realize that you *do not* have to instruct your child in this process. In fact, you *cannot* because the operations are implicit. How could any of us possibly guess or anticipate how another person's brain will make

Figure 6.1   The Predictive Cycle

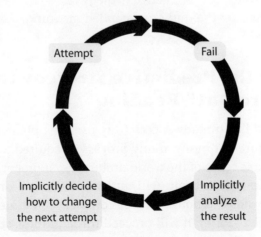

sense of text? We know that knowledge of the alphabet, knowledge of language and how it works, and sufficient knowledge of the topic are all necessary. We also know that the brain must be able to implement a predictive strategy, interpret visual input, focus attention, and perform executive functions. However, we don't know how each individual brain might choose to plan, coordinate, and integrate all of the information it needs to make sense of a specific printed message. The good news is that *we don't need to know.* For generations, determined children have taught themselves to be excellent readers, able to comfortably and easily make sense of an author's message. The brain, therefore, *doesn't need our help.* It is naturally equipped to engage in a predictive strategy to figure out the process *if* adults provide appropriate guidance and opportunities.

Encouraging Your Child to Use the Predictive Strategy

While you can't explicitly *tell* your child to experiment with books in order to figure out the passage-reading process, you can *encourage* your child in subtle ways to use a predictive strategy to figure it out. The two are significantly different. As you review the techniques on the following pages, be mindful that your job is to provide your child with subtle but meaningful guidance that will cause her to want to experiment implicitly with reading on her own. Doing too much to help her can actually get in the way of her ability to figure out the complex process for herself. The implicit nature of reading makes it impossible for you to know exactly what her brain needs to make reading happen, and, if the instructions you give are too specific, you may well provide her with the wrong information.

Just as it is impossible for you to know exactly what your child needs to develop excellent reading ability, it is also impossible for her to know, in an explicit sense, precisely what she needs to make reading happen. Her marvelous brain, however, is eminently capable of using the predictive strategy to implicitly figure it all out. Indeed, that's the only way it can happen. The techniques described in this chapter provide subtle ways through which you can encourage your child to use a predictive strategy to figure out the passage-reading process.

Techniques for Learning the Alphabet

Knowledge of letters and the sounds they represent is, of course, fundamental to the act of reading. As your child becomes an excellent reader, she will use her knowledge of the alphabet to keep predictions of an author's message coming and to confirm or reject the predictions as she makes them. Her brain must be free to choose alphabetic information from wherever it is in a given passage to make rapid predictions about the text. Fixating on every single letter or word in a sentence in sequential left-to-right order will cause reading to be slow and laborious. The highly efficient brain is capable of reading in a much faster way when it is free to seek and sample key alphabetic information.

The following techniques will help you encourage your child to develop appropriate alphabetic knowledge without sending the brain the erroneous message that it must use the alphabet for decoding or sounding out words.

Technique 1: Use Alphabet Books to Teach Sound-Symbol Associations

Use alphabet books with children who are prereaders as soon as they are old enough to enjoy having objects pointed out to them. Choose books that have a single letter in both capital (uppercase) and lowercase forms on a page along with numerous objects beginning with that letter. Simple ABC books with which children can entertain themselves by identifying objects can be "read" by children when they are very young. Remember, when your child chooses to spend time with this type of alphabet book, she is doing more than occupying her time. She is using the book to figure out the alphabetic principle—written symbols represent the sounds of spoken language, or, in less technical terms, the letter *B* says "buh," like the sound you hear at the beginning of the word *ball*. (See the list of recommended alphabet books in the Appendix.)

Alphabet books that involve stories rather than pictures of objects can be enjoyable for read-aloud activities, but they are not useful to a child who is in the beginning stages of figuring out the reading process. With these narrative books, she cannot look at the letter of focus (such as *D*), point to associated objects, and say, "Dog, drum, dinosaur."

Activity: "What's That?" (Objects). This is a great activity for your child because, in addition to providing her with useful information about the alphabet, it is increasing her stored knowledge about the names and nature of objects in her world. Point to objects in alphabet books and ask: "What's that?"

- If she doesn't know, tell her, and then ask again: "What's that?"
- If she does know, continue the activity by asking another question. Ask: "What else can you see on the page?" Or: "Can you find another animal (or toy, piece of fruit, etc.)?"

Without even being instructed, your child will begin to copy you and ask, "What's that?"

Activity: "What's That?" (Letters). While interacting with an alphabet book, point to the letter on a page as though it is just one more in the series of objects being pointed out (as, indeed, it is!) and ask: "What's that?"

- If she doesn't know, say: "That's the letter *B*. Can you say *B*?"

When she can consistently respond with, "*B*" or "That's a *B*," tell her that the letter *B* says "buh" and that everything on the page starts with the sound of the letter *B*. Conclude by pointing to each object and saying its name, emphasizing the "buh" sound. Once in a while, repeat the initial sound two or three times as you say the name of an object on the page. Say: "Buh, buh, buh—ball!"

After she has heard many times that *ball*, *basket*, *bird*, *bath*, and so on, all start with the letter *B*, start asking her what *ball* starts with.

- If she doesn't answer immediately, say: "Buh, buh, buh—ball."
- If she still doesn't say "*B*," tell her: "That's the letter *B*. *Ball* starts with the letter *B*."

Repeat with the other objects from the *B* page of the alphabet book.

Point to the letter *B* occasionally and, as you do, remind your child that the objects start with the letter *B*.

Technique 2: Emphasize the Reliable Letters

Some letters of the alphabet are more confusing than others. The letter *C*, for example, does not represent a unique sound; it represents the *S* sound (as in *city*) or the *K* sound (as in *cut*), or it joins with *H* to form the sound heard at the beginning and end of the word *church*. The letters *G* and *Y*, on the other hand, each represent two different sounds (*gun* and *germ*, *yellow* and *by*). Other letters can be confusing or difficult because of their limited occurrence in text (*V* and *Z*), their "unusualness" (*X* and *Q*), or their frequent connection with a "partner" (*Q* and *U*, *W* and *H*). Don't insist that your child know these confusing letters or letter combinations as she begins to make attempts at reading. She will, believe it or not, pick them up as she becomes increasingly engaged in experiments with reading. Her sharp little brain will notice that *Q* and *U* are almost always a team and that *W* and *H* frequently go together. As she begins to anticipate text, she'll notice that *C* and *H* appear in stories that involve a "church" or "cheese," and *T* and *H* show up in stories about "throwing" or "them."

Remember, excellent readers read by predicting an author's message, and the brain strategically samples the available letters in the process of predicting. This means that the brain doesn't have to know all of the letters. Because it is engaged in predicting, the brain can make the system work by mastering only the stable letters—those that consistently represent a single sound. Think about it: if you needed some additional information from the printed page, wouldn't it be more efficient to sample alphabetic information that is stable—or always the same—and therefore reliable? That's exactly what the brain does. And, as it does, the predictive strategy enables the brain to fill in the missing details. Your job is to help your child learn the stable parts of the alphabet and their corresponding sounds so she can figure out how to use the stable letters to make excellent reading happen. If she learns all of her letters and the corresponding sounds, good for her! If she doesn't, there is no need to pressure her to do so. Granted, the alphabet plays a key role in passage reading, but it does not play the most important role. That honor belongs to the predictive strategy.

Does that mean you should ignore some of the letters when you are reading alphabet books with your child? No, not necessarily. It means you should spend more time with the stable letters and less time with the confusing ones. There is no point in confusing your child when she is first figuring out the process of reading. If she does not easily grasp irregular letters, don't worry about it. The most useful and least confusing letters are these fourteen:

B, D, F, H, J, K, L, M, N, P, R, S, T, *and* V

Did you notice there are no vowels (*A, E, I, O, U*) in the list? All vowels are highly unpredictable in English. In one given word, a vowel or set of vowels may be pronounced one way, and in another word, the same vowel or set of vowels may have an entirely different pronunciation. A perfect example of this is the word *read*. Now, did I mean *read* as in "we are going to read" or did I mean *read* as in "we have already read"?

Vowels are not stable in the way that the sounds represented by letters such as *S* and *T* are stable, and sending an erroneous message that they are would be confusing to a child. When working with the *A, E, I, O,* and *U* pages of alphabet books, it might be best to focus only on objects that start with the long sounds of the vowels (such as *acorn, eraser, ice, oval,* and *unicorn*). Doing so will help reduce confusion.

Vowels aren't as necessary for reading as the other letters (the consonants) because their location in words is highly predictable. You experienced this in Chapter 2 when you read a list of vowel-less words and then a sentence containing those vowel-less words. As long as readers know where the vowels are going to be, usually between consonants, it doesn't matter what they are. As your child figures out how to make the predictive strategy work with reading, she will fill in the details correctly. Because she is appropriately focused on anticipating the passage's meaning, she will accurately anticipate sentences like these: "I can read! You can read! We all know what we read!"

Technique 3: Use Alphabet Magnets on the Refrigerator

Sets of alphabet letters that are magnetized and can be stuck to the refrigerator provide another opportunity to reinforce your child's growing knowledge of the alphabet. The activities in this section are appropriate to use after your child has learned some of the letters and their sounds. Be sure to begin by focusing on letters that she can recognize. This will ensure her success, thereby helping her feel a sense of pride in her accomplishment. Taking pride in what we can do helps fuel intent!

Activity: Identifying Letters. Place all of the letters on the refrigerator and ask your child, "Bring me a *B*," or any letter you are confident she knows.

- *If she gives you the right letter,* show her a place on the refrigerator where she can group all the letters she correctly identifies.

- *If she gives you the wrong letter*, coach her. For example, say: "No, that's not the letter *B*, but it kind of looks like it (only if it does, of course). That's the letter *D*. Do you want to try again to find the letter *B*, or do you want me to show you where it is?" Then comply with your child's wishes.

If you have more than one of the same letter on the refrigerator when you ask your child to find a specific letter, encourage her to keep looking until she finds all of them.

- *Say*: "Can you find more *B*s? Put all the ones you can find over here." Show her an available spot on the refrigerator to place all of the *B*s.
- *If she doesn't see them all*, encourage her further. Say to her: "I see another *B*. Can you find it?"

When she finishes the task, ask her to think of a word that begins with the letter she retrieved or grouped, or ask her if she sees anything in the room that begins with the letter. You can join in by offering words or identifying objects.

Activity: Identifying Sounds. This activity is an extension of the preceding activity. If your child knows some of the letters and the sounds they make, she is ready for this activity. Again, focus on the letters she already knows.

- *Say*: "Bring me a letter that makes the 'buh' sound."
- *Or*, if you have more than one of the same letter on the refrigerator, you can change your request and say to her: "Put all the letters that make the 'buh' sound over here."

When she finishes the task, ask her to think of a word that begins with the sound of the letter she retrieved, or ask her if she sees anything in the room that begins with the sound of the letter. Once again, you can join in by identifying objects.

If your child brings the wrong letter, coach her. For example, say: "No that's not the letter that makes the 'buh' sound. That letter makes the 'duh' sound. They kind of sound alike, don't they (only if they do, of course)? Do you want to try again to find the letter that makes the 'buh' sound, or do you want me to show you where it is?" Once again, comply with your child's wishes.

Technique 4: Play Alphabet Games

Inventing alphabet games is another way to reinforce your child's growing knowledge of the alphabet. Initiate activities like these as soon as she begins learning the names of the letters and their associated sounds.

Activity: Flash Card Find-a-Letter. Make or buy flash cards with single letters on them (a single capital letter on one side and the same letter in lowercase on the other side). Remember that capital letters and lowercase letters are significantly different, and your child needs to learn both. In this activity, be sure to include both cases. Put a few of the flash cards (no more than five, to conform with the limitations of short-term memory) on a table. Initially, put letters that are distinctly different in appearance together. As your child becomes more skilled at this activity, assemble letters that look more alike.

- *Ask*: "Can you find the letter *B*?" (or any letter she knows).
- *If she can't find the letter*, point it out for her and then name another letter in the set and ask her to find it. Return to the letter that gave her trouble later. Continue this activity until she becomes efficient at locating letters.

You can also increase the complexity by switching the focus to the sounds of the letters.

- *Say*: "Find the letter that makes the 'buh' sound."
- *Or*: "Find the letter that the word *ball* begins with."

Have fun with this activity, increasing the complexity by putting a greater number of letters on the table.

Activity: "I Spy." This fun activity involves a search for objects in your child's environment that begin with certain sounds. The focus, therefore, is entirely on sounds and not on the shapes of letters.

- Say: "I spy, with my little eye, something that begins with the letter *B*."
- When she gets it right, let her know and say: "That's right!"
- Every time she guesses a word that begins with a sound other than "buh," tell her. Say: "No, that doesn't begin with the letter *B*."
- If she guesses a word like *rug*, let her figure out that the two sounds are different. Say: "Buh, buh, buh—rug. That word begins with the 'ruh' sound: ruh, ruh, ruh—rug."
- If she guesses something that does begin with the letter *B* but it isn't what you have in mind, give her a cue that lets her know that, technically, she is right, but it isn't what you had in mind. Say: "That begins with *B*, all right, but it isn't what I spied."

Keep the activity interesting by alternating with something other than alphabet sounds. This will prevent an implicit message that you want her to learn the alphabet sounds. Some children, for whatever reason, don't like the idea that they are complying with your agenda. Say: "I spy, with my little eye, something that is blue."

Children who struggle with this activity may be more successful at first with colors that they already know rather than sounds. In this case, use colors at first until your child becomes comfortable with the activity, and then reintroduce the alphabet.

Two important goals of this activity are for it to be fun and for your child to experience success. Remember that feelings of pleasure and success support intent. Lack of pleasure or success can diminish intent. Also remember that you are providing your child with opportunities, but it is her choice whether or not to enter the arena. If she chooses not to, you can be assured that her brain is not ready to do so. Keep it light; keep it fun; follow her lead.

Activity: The Traveling Alphabet Game. While traveling, see who can identify the most objects starting with a particular letter of the alphabet (for example, *B*—for *building*). Everyone in the car can play (the driver with caution). Take turns identifying the letters that will be used.

A variation on this game when your child knows enough is to start at the beginning of the alphabet and look, in turn, for objects starting with *A, B, C, D, E, F*, and so on. The same object cannot be used by two players. Whoever gets to the end of the alphabet first, or is the furthest along in the alphabet when the game is disbanded, is the winner. Coach older brothers and sisters to help younger siblings, hesitating as needed to allow time for the younger child to find appropriate objects. Or, assign an older child to work with a younger child by coaching her where to look and occasionally whispering in her ear when an appropriate object appears.

Activity: "Which One Begins with *B*?" You can play this sound-identification game anywhere. It doesn't have to be a lengthy affair—you can ask a single question as you are walking upstairs to bed, or choose to play for just a few minutes in the park or doctor's office. Again, always follow your child's lead.

- Say: "*Table, ball, grass*. Which one begins with *B*?" Be sure to switch the order so that the *B* word is not always in the middle. Otherwise, her clever brain might figure out that *B* words always turn up in the middle of a three-word set. If she doesn't immediately respond, tell her the answer.
- When she is competent with a particular sound, make the activity a little more complex. Say: "*Table, bed, book*. What begins with *B*?"
- When she answers, "*Bed* and *book*," let her know that she is right. Exclaim: "I tried to fool you, but you were too smart!"

- If she names only one object, simply agree, and don't call attention to it. The fact that she could not name both objects is your signal that you "tried to fool her" too soon.

This game, like the others suggested, provides the brain the opportunity to figure out the sound-symbol correspondences of our system of written language. When mistakes are made, it is a signal to the brain that it has not completely "wired" the knowledge in correctly. Immediate feedback is called for. *Never* send your child any signals that you are disappointed when she makes any kind of mistakes, whether it be misidentifying the starting letter of an object or being unable to come up with a word that starts with a particular letter sound. The brain cannot learn without making mistakes. Expect them, and treat them matter-of-factly when they occur. In any of the games, switch roles with your child whenever you can by letting her ask *you* the questions.

Techniques for Using Predictable Books

As your child begins to learn the stable letters of the alphabet and the sounds they represent, it is time to begin the process of encouraging her to make attempts at reading with predictable books. Every child must make attempts at reading to figure out the implicit process, and it is essential that children continue to want to make those attempts (your child must maintain *intent* to figure out the complex reading process). It is your job to make sure that nothing is ever said or done to discourage your child from making attempts. The techniques that follow provide information that will help you. All of these techniques revolve around books that are easily predicted. They are predictable either because your child has heard the stories over and over (the stories are familiar) or because they are repetitive and limited in the scope of language (the text itself is inherently predictable). Wordless pic-

ture books are also inherently predictable because the pictures tell the story.

When a child is consistently exposed to books in which
the stories can be easily anticipated, the child's brain will be
more likely to experiment with the predictive strategy as it
strives to figure out how to make excellent reading happen.

Technique 1: Use Wordless Picture Books

Use wordless picture books to begin encouraging your child
to use a predictive strategy. The purpose of these books is to
convey meaning (or a message) through the pictures.

- First, you "read" the book to her by telling the story as it is
  told by the pictures. As you do, point out to her key visual
  information from each page.
- Next time the two of you sit down with the book, ask her to
  tell you the story, using the pictures as appropriate clues.
  Don't intervene in how she interprets the story, unless what
  she says has absolutely *nothing* to do with the picture on
  the page she is "reading."

Put yourself in the shoes of your child and try to make sense
of her interpretation. If you can't because she is completely off-
track, ask questions rather than correct her. For example:

- If the picture is about the beach and a beach ball, but she
  begins to tell a story about climbing a mountain, intervene.
  Say: "I don't see a mountain in this picture. Can you show
  me a mountain?"
- When she says no, continue to ask her questions. Say:
  "What is the picture about?"
- If she doesn't know, ask another question. Say: "What's
  that?" and point to the beach.
- If she says, "I don't know," or if she doesn't immediately
  answer, tell her what it is. Say: "It's a beach. Your story
  needs to have a beach in it. Do you want to tell me a different story about these pictures, or do you want me to tell
  you the story about the beach again?"

As always, let your child choose the next course of action to take.

Technique 2: Use Familiar Books to Encourage a Predictive Strategy

The more familiar a book is, the more easily your child will anticipate the author's message. Any book becomes familiar when you read it over and over to your child. Predictable books—books that make it easy to anticipate the text because they follow a pattern of language or because they involve concepts that we know well—are easy to anticipate and, as such, become familiar to us faster.

A book that my son wrote when he was five years old (with me acting as scribe) nicely illustrates this concept:

Hands [Every page is illustrated with his traced hand.]
Page 1: Hands can clap.
Page 2: Hands can wave.
Page 3: Hands can draw pictures.
Page 4: Hands can give you a present.
Page 5: Hands can tuck you in at night.
Last page: Hands can do all kinds of things.

Not only is the language in this story highly predictable, but also there is a limited amount of print on each page. The sparse text makes it easier for your child to look in the right place as she strives below the level of consciousness to figure out how to efficiently use alphabetic information to help with her predictions.

Young children love to hear the same stories read to them again and again. Why? Do they struggle to remember the story from one reading to the next? Highly unlikely. It is more likely that their brains are trying to figure out how books work and the process of passage reading. For this reason, it is important to read the same books to your child over and over. No matter how many times your child asks you to read the same story, follow her lead. She may be using one particular book to help her figure out the passage-reading process. If your child has no idea what a story says, how can she possibly figure out how the system of reading works? *She can't.*

Predictable books should be a regular part of a child's pre-reading experience. Read them to your child again and again. You might even tape-record yourself reading such books so your child can listen and follow along when you are not available. If she isn't asking for the same book over and over, make it a nightly ritual to read the same book at bedtime (perhaps in addition to a book your child chooses). *Goodnight Moon*, by Margaret Wise Brown (HarperTrophy, 1977), is an excellent choice for a predictable bedtime story.

Things to Avoid When Encouraging the Predictive Strategy

- **Avoid pressuring your child to engage in any of the activities in this chapter.** Remember: if your child isn't having fun, back off. I cannot say this enough. Frustration impedes a child's ability to "figure out" the reading process.
- **Avoid alphabet books that feature only one or two objects with each letter.** The brain needs multiple objects to learn letter sounds, and you do not want your child to move to the next letter too soon.
- **Don't rely on the "Alphabet Song" as a way to teach the alphabet.** The "Alphabet Song" can contribute to positive feelings around the alphabet, but it is not very helpful as a foundation for reading. It is the correspondence between written symbols and the sounds they represent that must be learned to aid in the process of reading. It is possible to be able to sing the "Alphabet Song" and not know how to identify any of the letters or to identify any of the associated sounds. Many kindergartens and preschools introduce this song to their students, so if your child knows it beforehand, it will boost her esteem when she goes to school—which is reason enough to introduce the song. It can be sung with other members of the family, it can be introduced from a CD or cassette, or you can sing it to her as you put her to bed or give her a bath. Invite her to sing along as best she

can, and eventually she will be able to perform for Grandma and Grandpa. Again, however, do not rely on the "Alphabet Song" as a prereading activity. It is not.

- **Never make your child feel that she has to learn all the letters of the alphabet or how to read in order to please you.** The learning will be comfortable and natural if you keep it casual and don't judge your child's progress. Celebrate learning and acknowledge authentic achievements by "showing Daddy" (or Grandma or whomever).
- **Never give your child "think time" to name letters or sounds.** Your child either knows a letter or sound or she doesn't. If she doesn't, tell her, in the moment, what the letter or sound is and move on with the fun activities that are designed to help her learn. Giving "think time" could make her feel as though she is being tested. Feeling tested is intimidating and may make her less likely to want to be involved.
- **Avoid anything that would draw your child's attention away from the message or meaning being conveyed by an author.** Focusing on meaning is essential to the reading process because all excellent readers read from meaning.
- **Don't force reading activities.** If you demonstrate an interest in alphabet books, magnetic letters, and predictable books, your child is likely to be interested, too. Encourage her involvement by modeling how interesting and fun the activities can be. Don't ever force her involvement in reading activities!

Success Story: A Timber Worker and Hundreds of Others Become Excellent Readers

Using a predictive strategy to figure out how to improve reading performance is powerful stuff. It works not only for children just learning to read but also for individuals diagnosed with dyslexia.

continued

As a high school student more than twenty years ago, Ken Reinertsen was diagnosed with severe dyslexia by clinicians at the University of California, Los Angeles. He attended that university's prestigious Fernald Reading Clinic for more than a year and developed reading ability in a second-grade range. However, when he graduated from public high school, he was still reading at a second-grade level.

As an adult, Ken chose a job with a timber company in part because the job didn't require reading. In 1990, his employer—Simpson Timber Company—began a pilot literacy program as part of a project to prepare employees for new technology. The company examined a variety of adult literacy programs being used across the United States and chose READ RIGHT® because it was significantly different in its approach from any other reading program that Simpson's employees had encountered in school. At the start of the project, Ken was assessed. It was found that he inserted words that rendered what he was reading meaningless, dropped endings from words, and omitted key portions of what he was reading. The severity of Ken's reading problem resulted in his initial placement in the program in first-grade-level books. After only sixty hours of tutoring, Ken read well enough to read his first novel, *Where the Red Fern Grows*, by Wilson Rawls. After a total of ninety-nine hours of tutoring, he was reading at a post-high-school level with ease, comfort, and total understanding. Even before completing the program, Ken began reading management books such as *The One-Minute Manager, The Art of Leadership,* and *Better Makes Us Best.*

Based on success with Ken and nineteen other timber workers, Simpson's pilot literacy project was deemed a success, and over the next five years, the program was expanded to seventeen other Simpson sites in seven states: Washington, Oregon, California, Michigan, Pennsylvania, Vermont, and Texas. A review of data kept for the project shows that Simpson tutors delivered 17,654 hours of tutoring and reported 1,998 grade levels of gain. This success was possible because READ RIGHT methodology compelled the struggling readers to use a predictive strategy to figure out how to make excellent reading happen.

The predictive strategy involves implicit experimentation by the brain. Regardless of whether we are talking about children or adults, if the brain doesn't experiment, it doesn't learn.

7

Coaching Your Child to Excellent Reading Ability

Imagine what it must have been like four hundred years ago to gaze up at the afternoon sky and be certain that the earth beneath your feet was the center of the universe. This was the accepted belief in Galileo's time. The sun and the planets revolved around Earth, and Earth was the center of life.

But Galileo carefully observed the sky through his newly built telescope and discovered evidence that Earth revolved around the sun. When Galileo begged to differ with the authorities of his time based on this new scientific evidence, he was put on trial and placed under house arrest for the remainder of his life!

Common sense told well-meaning people centuries ago that the sun revolved around Earth. Earth *must be* stationary, they assumed, because it doesn't feel as if it is moving. Today, nearly everyone in the world accepts the scientific fact that Earth is part of a solar system and that Earth revolves around the sun.

The Greatest Obstacle to Reading Success

Where reading is concerned, the accepted belief among most well-meaning people of today is that reading revolves around the words on a page. Common sense tells them that focusing on and identifying each and every word is the path to excellent reading ability. Right?

Wrong! Welcome to the greatest obstacle in the process of guiding your child to excellent reading ability. Your effectiveness as a coach on this journey all comes down to daily make-or-break moments that will arise again and again. To be effective, you must constantly suppress your natural tendency and desire to direct your child's focus to decoding and otherwise identifying each and every word on a page. Why? As I've said before, the key to excellent reading ability does not center on identifying words. Instead, it is centered on the appropriate construction and use of neural circuitry in our brains to anticipate or predict an author's intended message. Passage reading, therefore, revolves around grounding everything we read—from the moment reading begins—in *meaning* and not the identification of each and every word. The faulty belief that identifying words is the foundational skill that must be mastered to become an excellent reader is probably the single most common cause of reading problems.

Well-meaning parents and others who slip into focusing on word identification while working with children often say things such as the following:

- "Let's read a story. Do you want to take a turn, too? OK? This time, you read *the words*."
- "You didn't read that right. Look at *that word* again."
- "What did you say *that word* was?"
- "Sound out *that word*."
- "Sound it out."

These common interactions with children who are just learning to read are strictly taboo in the new view of reading presented throughout this book. Every year in various school learning centers, as my company trains tutors in the new view and its related methodology, we encounter well-meaning adults who find it hard to let go of these phrases. We consistently find that tutors who use them are far less effective than those who never use them at all. Such phrases may help children figure out the words in an unfamiliar list of words—but reading words individually is not the same cognitive act as passage reading.

The taboo phrases can prevent children from making appropriate discoveries about the complex, integrated process of truly excellent passage reading. To learn to read with excellence, your child must figure out how to anticipate the author's message, just as you did in several of the activities in Chapter 2. Children can do this only if they base a predictive strategy on the relevant knowledge they have already stored in their brains and then read *from* that knowledge (or *meaning*), never from the laborious identification of separate and disconnected words.

Lessons from the Rosetta Stone: The Importance of Using Familiar Books

To figure out the reading process independently, your child must become highly familiar with a select set of books. He needs that familiarity to figure out how the printed symbol system assists and supports the process of understanding an author's message.

An intriguing historical event demonstrates the importance of knowing the content of a message in advance. By the fourth century, the ability to read Egyptian hieroglyphics had been lost. Modern-day archaeologists and linguists could not determine how the mysterious written symbol system worked to communicate meaning.

In the late 1700s, however, during the construction of a fort in Egypt, one of Napoleon's soldiers made a fateful discovery: a stone inscribed with three scripts. The first script was identified by linguists as Egyptian hieroglyphics, the second was identified as a more common form of written Egyptian language (demotic script), and the third was identified as Greek. Linguists determined that the demotic and Greek scripts each communicated the same message, so they assumed that the third inscription on what soon came to be known as the Rosetta stone probably said the same thing. Knowing the common message enabled linguists to finally figure out the lost language of hieroglyphics!

Linguists had tried for centuries to figure out hieroglyphics, but they couldn't do it until they knew in advance what one particular message said. The same is true for your child. Your son or daughter won't be able to figure out how printed language works without knowing in advance what a message of interest says. So, no matter how often your child asks you to read the same book and no matter how much you may think, "If I have to read that book one more time, I'll go stark raving mad!" just grit your teeth, put on a happy face and a warm and inviting smile, and read the same book again. On a subconscious level, your child may be using the familiar story to figure out the reading process.

Once children implicitly understand the relationship between spoken language and a printed message, they will be able to figure out how to use that knowledge and all relevant information stored in the memory to anticipate and construct an author's intended message—the essence of what we call comprehension.

It sounds complex. It *is* complex—but the human brain possesses awesome capability to figure it all out, as evidenced by preschool-age children who do so every year. This chapter will introduce you to six categories of books along with flexible techniques for using them in a way that will make your child's job of "figuring it all out" much easier. First, let's look at three important foundational techniques to guide your interactions with your child (in these examples, a son), regardless of the type of book you use.

General Techniques for Coaching Excellent Reading Ability

Your job as your child's most important coach is to create excitement around reading, answer his questions, and gently nudge him toward making new discoveries for himself about how the reading process works. The following techniques are designed to help you accomplish those goals. These activities are more complex than they may initially appear. I suggest that you read through them thoughtfully and, as you begin interacting with your child, focus on perfecting one activity at a time. Periodically, read through all of the techniques and activities in Chapters 4 through 7, and conduct a mental check to make sure you are applying them appropriately. Remember that you, yourself, need to build a neural network to guide your child appropriately through these activities. Building neural networks is what the brain is designed to do, and it takes time!

Technique 1: Read from All Kinds of Books

In addition to reading the simple books we will discuss later in this chapter, you should regularly read aloud for pure pleasure from award-winning children's literature and any other book that holds your child's interest—including classics such as *Charlotte's Web* and *The Velveteen Rabbit*. You will find lists of classics and recommended read-aloud books in sources such as *The Read-Aloud Handbook*, by Jim Trelease, and *The Newbery and Caldecott Awards: A Guide to the Medal and Honor Books*, published by the American Library Association, both of which are listed in the Appendix. The Newbery and Caldecott Medals are awarded annually to books judged to be the best for children.

When choosing a book from these lists, consider your child's interests. He is more likely to be enthusiastic about reading if you choose subjects that are of interest to him. Hearing works of literature read to him will expand his knowledge of the world and language on multiple levels, both above and below the level of consciousness. Language-rich books may not be as useful to your child in his early reading attempts, but exposure to them will increase his knowledge of language and the world, and he will also be aware of the wide variety of literature available to him once he finally figures out how to read with excellence.

Technique 2: Always Respond to Your Child's Questions and Requests

Questions and requests to you from your child about all things associated with reading are important. They signal that he is taking charge of his own reading development on an implicit level. It is of the utmost importance, therefore, that you always answer his questions about reading-related activities and, as best you can, fulfill his requests. You can never know what cognitive puzzle he is seeking to solve.

Questions that your child may ask will be specific to a particular book. Let's consider the questions a very young child might ask about a common childhood story such as *The Tale of Peter Rabbit*. If you live in a city, he might point to the garden in the story and ask: "What's that?" After you tell him: "That's a garden," if he has never seen a garden before, he may ask: "What's a garden?" Or, he may simply ask again: "What's that?" referring to the concept of a garden. Your job is to explain that a garden is where things such as fruits, vegetables, or flowers grow. In this way, you've just expanded your child's knowledge of the world. He will file this important information away in memory, ready to be used in the future to make sense of stories you read to him or stories he eventually tries to figure out for himself.

In another example using Peter Rabbit, you may get to the part in the story when the farmer wants to catch Peter, and, if your child has enough language ability to express his concerns, he may want to know why the farmer wants to hurt Peter. It is your job to explain to him that, when rabbits eat vegetables in a garden, some people don't like it, so they will do whatever they can to keep the rabbits out of their gardens. Once again, this will provide your child with more knowledge about his world that he will use at a later time. In this case, you've provided him with the concept that cuddly creatures sometimes pose problems for people. This little piece of information that many of us take for granted is an important concept that will be useful to a child throughout life—including for activities such as reading, in which he needs to anticipate what it is an author is attempting to communicate based on what he already knows about the world.

Requests your child will make about reading will be simple and could involve any request related to a book. Examples of requests from a very young child include the following:

- "Read that one, Daddy."
- "Now this one, Mommy."
- "I want another bunny book."
- "Read it again."

Such requests reflect more than your child's interest in books. They are evidence of a developing interest in figuring out the reading process. Do everything you can to comply with his requests so that he has everything he needs to figure it out.

Technique 3: Be Sensitive to Your Child's Signals

It is imperative that you develop a sensitivity to the signals your child sends as to when it is OK to go ahead with any reading-related activity and when it is time to back off. You may undermine his intent if you try to push him when he's not interested. Pushing him may result in sending the self-defeating message that your child "can't do it." He can! But he has to do it on *his* time schedule, not yours. It is essential that you be patient and follow your child's lead.

The Six Categories of Books

The activities in this section are designed to help you follow your child's lead. They focus on six categories of simple children's books your child will use to figure out the reading process for himself. The Appendix provides a list for each category.

1. Simple ABC books
2. ABC read-aloud books
3. Wordless and almost wordless picture books

4. Highly predictable books
5. Predictable books
6. Minimal-print early readers

These books do not represent "levels" that you will use to guide your child through a series of steps. Instead, once you introduce each category to your child, you will use books from any category that seems appropriate at any given time. Keep in mind that it is impossible for you to know exactly what your child needs to figure out how to make reading happen. It is imperative, therefore, that you provide an environment in which he can pick and choose what is most useful to him. For example, whether he expresses an interest in an ABC book or a predictable book depends on the level of his accumulated knowledge, his language ability, and what kind of information he needs to continue his implicit quest to figure out the complex process of passage reading. Allow him to take the lead in choosing books.

If your child is using single words or two- or three-word sentences to communicate, he may enjoy simple ABC books the most because he possesses enough language ability to interact with them and because he has not yet learned to associate written symbols with sounds of language. Older children may not enjoy simple ABC books as much because they already know what all the objects in the books are and feel they know their ABCs. They may, consequently, prefer stories. It will be a mixed bag. There is no precise formula for the "ages and stages" when a child will express an interest in any type of book. Your job is to follow your child's lead and to judge what he is ready for by his performance.

How you use the books is far more important than which specific book you use. As you consider each of these techniques, some information may seem familiar to you because it was mentioned in previous chapters. That's good! The more familiar you are with this information, the more likely you are to use it correctly and the more likely you are to become an excellent coach for your child.

Technique for Using Simple ABC Books

From birth, children should be exposed to a variety of books for pure enjoyment but also in preparation for reading development. As soon as your child is old enough to sit on your lap by himself, introduce him to alphabet books through the techniques described in Chapter 6. If he isn't yet old enough to mimic you as you say the names or make the sounds of the letters, just "read" the alphabet books to him and point out the objects. In addition to helping children figure out the associations between letters of the alphabet and the sounds they represent, simple ABC books are excellent for very young children for another reason: they are an enjoyable place for them to begin to explore the world of books.

Not only do alphabet books contain a wealth of wonderful information about letters, but through the sounds that the letters represent and depictions of objects in a child's world, they also provide a simple environment where your child can build a foundation to figure out how reading works. Almost everything he needs is there: the book, the meaning, the objects of interest, and the opportunity to begin to establish a relationship between oral language and the written symbol system.

Simple alphabet books with a targeted letter and several objects that start with the letter featured on a page can be "read" immediately and successfully by children ages eighteen months and up who are rapidly developing language abilities. Long before they can read, children can recognize pictures of "ball," "bat," and "bicycle" on a page, and as you show them how simple alphabet books work, they'll come to understand that the letter on the page represents the sound heard at the beginning of each word. As they use these books, they will begin to anticipate that all the objects on a page begin with a certain letter, giving them the opportunity to figure out for themselves the sound-symbol system.

Guide Your Child to Ask, "What's That?"

One of the very first questions your child likely will ask you when an alphabet book *or any other book with pictures* is in your hands or his is, "What's that?" Don't take the question lightly! Through these two simple words, he is inviting you to teach him about the world. His inquisitive mind is telling you that he is ready and eager to go. Keep this thought in the front of your mind as you begin the process of guiding him toward excellent reading ability. The more he asks, "What's that?" the better.

Until your child figures out the passage-reading process (and often even after), expect him to point to objects in any book and ask what they are. Always show your interest, and always answer. By doing so, you are helping him build knowledge of the world. Answering his questions also will help him know that he can rely on you as he seeks to figure out how communication through printed language works. Rather than grow weary of this question, cherish it. See it for what it really is: your child's filing away important information in gray matter, ready and waiting to be accessed as he seeks to figure out the complex process of passage reading.

Technique for Using ABC Read-Aloud Books

From a child's point of view, there is a great deal of difference between a simple ABC book and an ABC read-aloud book. The first is all about the identification of objects, and the second usually involves a story. From an adult's point of view, the goal of a simple ABC book is to show a child the relationship between a letter of the alphabet, the sound it represents, and the beginning sound of objects that should be familiar to him. Quite differently, the goal of an ABC read-aloud book is to share a story with a child in conjunction with what is often elaborate artwork. The two serve different purposes, and only one is best suited to helping a child develop reading ability on his own.

Elaborate, story-oriented alphabet books are appropriate as a read-aloud activity for children as young as one year. Use them just as you would classic children's stories—to read and enjoy and to discuss the characters or objects. However, do not rely on them to help your child figure out the alphabetic principle. That job is best left to simple ABC books that feature a letter of the alphabet and several objects on each page.

Technique for Using Wordless and Almost Wordless Picture Books and "Talking the Story"

Wordless picture books have no text at all and force the "reader" to tell or talk the story. Almost wordless picture books have few words, so the "reader" must tell or talk part of the story. "Talking" a story is an important early read-aloud strategy. It helps communicate to your child that books are about the fun and interesting messages authors are attempting to communicate, and it helps them know that the pictures are an integral source of information to help them anticipate an author's message. Remember, books are about the meaning they are intended to convey, not about individual words. Wordless and almost wordless picture books convey this fact wonderfully.

Use the "Talk the Story" strategy with standard picture books. Silently read a page at a time in advance, and then summarize for your child what is on the page. Pictures in picture books also can be used to involve your child in the story.

For example, a picture of a cow jumping over the moon provides you with such an opportunity.

- Point to the picture and say: "Look! There's the cow. What's he jumping over?"
- When your child answers correctly, or when you tell him the answer, you could say: "Do you think the cow could really jump over the moon?" [He answers.]
- Say to him: "Could you jump over the moon?" [He answers again.]

- Say to him: "I'll bet you could jump over other things, though. Do you want to show me how you can jump over something?"

Use the pictures to help introduce new information. For example:

- Say: "Did you know that milk comes from cows?"
- Then when he answers, point to the picture and ask him: "Did you know that the sac right there is where the milk comes from?"

See what wonderful opportunities to expand your child's knowledge of the world come from talking through books, rather than simply reading them?

Here is an example from another story. You read, "The elephant walked slowly." If you suspect that your child does not yet know what it is to walk slowly, it is a perfect time to engage your child in a discussion like this one:

- Ask him: "Where's the elephant?"
- After he points to the animal—or, if he can't, after you point it out—say: "If we use our fingers to walk like an elephant across the book, can you show me how an elephant would walk 'slowly'?"
- When he has demonstrated this for you (or, if he doesn't know, demonstrate for him and then encourage him to do it), ask him: "And what would our fingers do if the elephant walks 'fast'?"
- Again, give him a moment to demonstrate for you. If he can't, show him the concept of "fast" with your fingers.

Follow your child's lead in deciding whether to "read" a story or "talk" the story. If you start to read the book and he's not interested (he walks away, tries to get down, or starts playing with the book), it's a signal that he may not yet have the ability to string narration together. This is when you want to "talk" the story. Talking a story rather than reading it helps get your child personally involved in the story so that his interest remains high. If he is interacting with you as you talk through the story, he will be answering your questions, pointing to the pictures on cue, and often acting gleeful because he is fully engaged and obviously enjoying the process. This is exactly what you want to happen. Without exception, you want early reading experiences to capture your child's interest.

Techniques for Using Highly Predictable Books

Among the book lists in the Appendix, you will find one for highly predictable books. These are simple books that repeat the same phrases over and over, usually altering only the ends of the sentences. Use these books to interact with your child in his initial attempts at figuring out reading. Let your child guide you when he is ready for these books. You will know whether he is ready if you use the activities that follow and your child readily participates. If he doesn't, then he is not ready, and you should continue to read to him regularly from all kinds of books, including highly predictable ones, simple ABC books, and wordless and almost wordless picture books.

Assemble a collection of highly predictable books, and ask your child to choose the one he wants to read. By limiting the choice to highly predictable books, both you and your child have control over the activity—you control the type of book he is choosing, and he chooses the actual book. We all tend to have stronger intent when we feel we have a measure of control over an activity.

Technique 1: Coach Your Child to Read the Most Predictable Parts of the Sentence

Familiarize your child with the book and its repetitive patterns by reading it aloud to him again and again. As you read to your child, always sit so he can see the print, but there is no need to call his attention to it. You can read the book more than once in a single sitting if he will let you, or you can read it frequently over two or three days.

Invite his participation by encouraging him to "read" the predictable parts. To illustrate this point, look at the following example of text that could be found in a highly predictable book about people:

Page 1: People like to eat.
Page 2: People like to take walks.
Page 3: People like to take trips in the car.
Page 4: People like to go to movies.
Page 5: People like to hug their children.
Last page: Some people like to go to work!

Once you know that your child is familiar with the story because he has heard it several times (whether in a single day or over a period of days), read the first page, and before going to the next, say: "How is the next page going to start?"

- *If he gives the right answer* (such as, "People," "People like," "People like to," or even, "People like to take walks"), say: "Let's see." Turn the page, read it out loud, and say: "You're right! How did you know that?" You're not really looking for an answer to the question. Asking is a way of interacting with your child. Give a brief response and ask: "How is the next page going to start?" Your child will get it right again.
- *If he gives a wrong answer*, say: "Let's see." Turn the page and say: "You were close," or, "Nope." Without any further comment, read the page to him.
- *If he says he doesn't know*, say: "Let's see." Turn the page and, without any further comment, read the page to him. Read the book several more times before you ask him to participate again.
- *If he doesn't immediately answer*, don't provide think time. He either knows or doesn't know. Ignore the fact that he

hasn't responded. Say: "Let's see." Turn the page and keep reading. You may choose to point out pictures or discuss pictures with him as an aid to generating a prediction. Read the book *several more times* before you ask him to participate again.

Encourage your child to read the repetitive language on every page of a book. This may take one day or several days. Follow his lead, and don't try to rush through. Instead, if he begins to falter or lose interest, step in and read the rest of the story to him. He will benefit from interacting with the same story over and over. If he loses interest, you can choose to simply read stories to him for several days and return to working with this book later, or you might try the same technique with another highly predictable book that has repetitive language.

Technique 2: Coach Your Child to Read the Less Predictable Parts of the Sentence

Once your child can easily and comfortably anticipate the most predictable part of the text, focus his attention on the less predictable parts. There are two variations for doing this:

1. You read the predictable part to your child.
2. Your child "reads" the predictable part to you.

It doesn't matter which variation you use. You may choose to switch back and forth, or you and your child may prefer one variation over the other. Either way, the goal is to have him anticipate the unpredictable part of the sentence and follow up by "reading" the entire sentence.

You Start the Reading. If you elongate the word just before the place you want your child to read, he will readily catch on to this signal and eventually begin to fill in the rest of the sentence automatically every time you elongate a word. If he doesn't immediately answer, draw his attention to the picture.

- *You read*: "People like tooo . . ." and say: "Look at the picture. What do you think the people on this page like to do?"
- *He says*: "Eat!"—or whatever correctly anticipates the author's message. You say: "Yes! Now I bet you can read this page all by yourself! Do you want to try?"
- *If he says no*, read the page to him. Say: "Let's try the next page. People like tooo . . ." Continue with all the pages in the book in this manner.
- *If he says yes*, let him "read" the page to you. Say: "Do you think you can read the next one?" This will be his cue to try to do the next page on his own.

Coach him through each page, starting him out if necessary by saying: "People . . ." or, if he doesn't chime in, "People like to . . ." Draw his attention to each picture if he needs additional help to anticipate the author's message.

Your Child Starts the Reading. This variation gives your child the opportunity to demonstrate that he knows how to predict the predictable parts, while nudging him toward mastering the less predictable parts. Getting him started is easy.

- Ask: "How does the next page start?"
- When he predicts: "People like to . . ." and pauses, say: "Look at the picture. What do you think people like to do?"
- If he predicts: "Eat," then say: "Yes! Can you read the whole page?" Then say, "Let's read another page."

Continue having him read each page, drawing his attention to the pictures as needed. If he chooses not to read a page, you read it to him. As he "reads" parts of sentences or entire pages by himself, he may change the text. If he has the right idea but doesn't use the exact language the author used, *don't* intervene unless the sentence he produces makes no sense, sounds awkward, or radically changes the meaning. Use this example as the proper way to respond:

If the text says, "People like to eat," and your child reads, "People like to eat dinner," *don't* intervene. The change to the text does not radically change the author's meaning.

If, however, he reads, "People like to have a party," he has radically changed the author's meaning, and it is time to intervene.

- Tell him: "That didn't work. Read it again."
- If his text changes are still not acceptable, say: "Try once more."
- After his third attempt, you read the page to him.

Occasionally, read the entire book to him even when he has already figured out how to read it. This will give him an opportunity to notice any significant deviations he may be making and will give him an opportunity to "check out" any implicit understandings he may be forming about reading.

Technique 3: Set an Expectation for Excellence

When your child reads to you, judge whether he read with excellence, and provide honest feedback. This may be difficult for parents who are accustomed to praising a child whether or not the child has performed a task with excellence. Bear in mind that your reaction to your child's reading will influence his perception of what is and is not excellent. It is imperative that you help him figure out how to accurately judge his own reading. He has to come to know when he is achieving excellence and when he is not.

If your child achieves excellence, he will sound natural. As he reads, you will feel comfortable. When this happens, say either of the following:

- "Great! You sounded totally natural. That was excellent reading."
- "Great job! You sounded totally natural. Did you feel comfortable while you were reading?"

Or simply say: "That was excellent."

When he reads a sentence excellently, you might choose to have him read it a few more times to reinforce what excellent reading feels like.

If he doesn't achieve excellence, he will not sound natural. As he reads, you will feel uncomfortable. When this happens, try the following:

- Say: "Read that again so it feels more comfortable."
- Or say: "Read that again. It didn't sound natural."
- If it still isn't natural, say: "Try again." If yet again it isn't natural, say: "Once more."

If he achieves excellence, or if after three attempts he cannot achieve excellence, move on to the next page or on to another activity. Whatever you do, don't tell him he did a "good job" if his reading does not sound totally natural. Be accurate, consistent, and persistent. It is important that your child's brain knows when it reads with excellence and when it does not.

It is also important for your child to consistently "read" with excellence so that he does not become confused about what he is trying to achieve. If he displays a pattern of reading that is unnatural (not like conversational speech), you need to help him achieve excellence by enhancing the predictability of the text. Choose one sentence he has not read with excellence and try the following:

- Say: "I'm going to read this sentence to you, and then I want you to read it to me. OK?"
- Read the sentence to your child, and then say: "OK, your turn." Continue in this manner until he achieves excellence.
- For each time that his read isn't excellent, simply say: "No, that wasn't excellent. I'll read it to you again."
- After you read the sentence, say: "Now it's your turn."
- When the reading is excellent, say: "Yes! That was excellent." Move to a new page and repeat the interaction if you choose, or switch to a different activity.

Another way to make the text more predictable so your child can read it with excellence is to try the following:

- Say: "Why don't you read this sentence to me again and again until you feel totally comfortable? OK?"
- Each time that his read isn't excellent, say: "No, read it again," or, "Again."
- When the read is excellent, say: "Yes! That was excellent."

Technique 4: Help Your Child Learn to Judge Excellence

Once you have established a pattern of telling your child whether or not his reading was excellent, and he is consistently achieving excellence, begin to occasionally ask him if his reading was excellent. Say: "Was it excellent?"

When he answers, you agree or disagree and then continue with the reading activity you are applying. As your child becomes more proficient at judging his own excellence, continue to ask the same question. Be alert for patterns of inaccurate judging. When they occur, help him achieve excellence, and resume telling him when his reading is excellent and when it is not until he once again displays a pattern of consistently achieving excellence.

Technique 5: Create Opportunities for Your Child to Repeatedly Reread Books He Has Mastered

Once he can "read" an entire book comfortably by himself, turning pages at the appropriate times, celebrate by having him read it to everyone in the household and everyone who is willing to listen—Grandma and Grandpa, uncles and aunts, neighbors, and any visitors. Your child can even read over the telephone. If there are younger siblings, ask him to read to them to help you out so you can get the laundry folded or whatever.

Here's another nice way to honor and respect what your child has accomplished. When you and he sit down to read together, start out by having him read to you a book or a few pages he has already mastered. Say: "You did such a good job reading yesterday. Why don't you read that book to me again?"

Technique 6: Know How to Be an Effective Coach

The following information is intended to make you the best coach you can be, regardless of what category of book you are using or what specific technique you choose to use.

Understand That Reading and Memorizing Are "First Cousins." With many of the activities, you may be thinking, "Isn't my child just memorizing the text? How is that going to help him learn to read?" He may be memorizing the text, but strike the word *just*. Memorizing and reading both require prediction. We must predict in order to recite, and we must predict in order to read. In both cases, prediction requires efficient location of information stored in the brain and results in the effective reconstruction of the intended message. The difference, however, is that something that is memorized is 100 percent predictable, and something that is being read is not—some strategic information from the text is required to correctly anticipate the meaning. So, if your child is reciting, celebrate! It tells you that he implicitly understands the role of prediction in reading—efficient access to memory and effective reconstruction of any type of message.

Always Follow Your Child's Lead. Never force your child to participate in any activity around reading. Doing so can undermine intent. If he doesn't want to read a sentence over and over until he achieves excellence, move on. If he doesn't want to read the book on which you have been working, let him choose a different one. You can wait for another day to continue work on the one you would have chosen. If he doesn't want to read a book to Daddy or Grandma, don't make a big deal out of it.

Remain Cheerful in the Face of Your Child's Mistakes. When you're interacting with your child, make sure that your attitude is cheerful and positive, and expresses subtle confidence that he is going to be able to do what you are asking him to do. Remain neutral if your child makes a mistake or can't respond. Never register disappointment or exasperation. Don't set your child up for failure by saying something like: "I'll bet you can tell me how the next page will start," or, "I know you can read this next page," unless you are certain he can. Remember, your child has to want to read the book and participate. Otherwise, you may undermine his intent. If he's feeling as if he failed, he won't want to read the book on which you're working—or maybe he won't want to read at all.

Don't Provide Think Time. Either your child knows the answer to the question you are asking or he doesn't. Either he can do what you ask him to do or he can't. Waiting for a response tells him that you expect him to be able to give one. Keep it fun and casual.

Be Prepared to Take Over the Reading if Your Child Falters. If you ask your child to read a page or part of a page and you get no response, or he resists, immediately rescue him by reading it for him. You do not want him to feel as if he's failing. Make your *rescues* seamless so that your child interprets your response as simply how the activity works. You will eventually make it an undisrupted, seamless event. Your child will never experience or even anticipate frustration with the activity.

Never Call Your Child's Attention to Individual Words. Never, ever say anything like: "No, look at the words"; "Read that word again"; "You got every word right except that one. Good job!"; or, the biggest taboo of all, "Sound it out." Remember that the focus is not on the words. It is on your child's ability to accurately construct the author's message. All of these activities are designed to encourage your child to implicitly experiment with a predictive strategy so he can successfully anticipate the author's intended message. Don't confuse the message by drawing his attention to words or decoding. He must figure out for himself how to strategically sample the alphabetic information to make the predictive strategy work. Never suggest what he should do to make excellent reading happen.

Don't Intervene if He Makes a Change in the Language of the Text—as Long as It Works. An excellent reader frequently changes the author's language, but the change is always acceptable and logical. The sentence still makes sense, is not awkward, and doesn't radically change the author's meaning. This may be difficult for you to execute because it contradicts what most people assume about reading—that it is all about the identification of each and every word. But again, reading is not about the words; it is about anticipating an author's intended message. Your goal is to encourage your child to accurately predict what the author is conveying—not to correctly identify each and every word on a page. Your child's brain will figure out reading correctly as long as you don't try to tell him how to accomplish it.

Always Be Aware of Your Job as a Coach. You should regard every technique and activity as a tool to help you do your job as a coach. Your job is to do the following:

- Ensure that your child has a correct concept of excellent reading.
- Help your child come to know when he is achieving excellence and when he is not.
- Hold your child accountable for achieving excellence while simultaneously transferring the accountability to him. He must know for himself when he is achieving excellent reading and when he is not, and he must maintain strong intent to achieve it.
- Interact with your child and the text in such a way that he *can* achieve excellence.

The only way your child will ever be able to achieve excellence is if he forms, on an implicit level, a link between what he already knows and the author's message. Enhancing the predictability of the text enables him to establish this link. You, as your child's coach, must do whatever you need to do to make the text predictable enough so your child will anticipate the author's message. If you consistently do so, your child will understand that the job of the reader is to predict the message, and he will figure out exactly how to make the implicit predictive strategy work. He will become an excellent reader.

Techniques for Using Predictable Books

As soon as your child (regardless of age) is having consistent and quick success interacting with highly predictable books, begin including "predictable books" in your reading activities. You can choose from the list in the Appendix. Introduce and use these books following the same activities as those described for the highly predictable books. In a few cases, the activities are applied to predictable books a little differently, and sometimes additional activities are required to help your child continue his progress. As discussed before:

- Assemble a collection of predictable books, and ask your child to choose the one he wants to read.
- Familiarize him with the book and its repetitive patterns by reading it aloud to him again and again.
- Invite his participation by encouraging him to "read" the predictable parts.

With predictable books, inviting his participation will be a little different because every page is not highly predictable. If you are following the activities as outlined, you will have already read the book several times to your child before you invite him to read, and your initial invitation will be for your child to read *only* the highly predictable pages as you read all of the other pages.

Technique 1: Expand the Activity to Include the Less Predictable Parts of the Sentence

As your child demonstrates his success with the highly predictable pages, occasionally invite him to read the less predictable ones. You can help enhance the predictability by prompting your child regarding how to use information from the pictures and his knowledge of the world to anticipate the meaning of nonpredictable pages. The following examples will help.

If the text says, "The little boy put on his coat and went outside," you say: "On this page, the little boy wants to go outside, but look out the window of his house. There's snow! It's cold out there. I think he'll need to put a coat on before he goes out, don't you?"

- If he answers yes, say: "Read this," and point to the sentence.
- If he hesitates, prompt him: "Who are we talking about here?"
- If he can't answer, tell him: "The little boy. Go ahead and read it."

If he still hesitates, say: "The littlll . . ." [Elongate the last sound.]

- Your child says: "The little boy [and pauses]."
- You say: "What is the little boy doing?"
- Your child says: "Putting on his coat."
- You say: "That's right. Read it."
- Your child says: "The little boy is putting on his coat [pause]."
- You say: "What did the little boy do after he put on his coat? The picture doesn't show it, but what did he do?"
- Your child says: "Went outside."
- You say: "Yes. Now you can read the whole thing."
- Your child reads: "The little boy put on his coat [pause]."
- You say: "and . . ."
- If your child doesn't chime in, say: "and weeent . . . [elongate]."

- Your child says: "Outside!"
- You say: "Yes. The little boy put on his coat and went outside. Now you read it."

As you work more and more with less predictable books, you will need to provide fewer and fewer prompts. Whenever you sense that your child is getting "bogged down," intervene by reading the sentence to him, and then ask him to read it back to you.

Technique 2: Summarize Key Points

Another activity to increase the predictability of the text is to summarize the key points of what has already been read.

It might sound something like this: "Remember, this little duck has been looking for his mommy. He looked under a rock; he looked behind the barn; he looked in the chicken house. But he couldn't find his mommy, so he feels sad. This page tells you what he did because he feels so sad. Look at the picture. Now read it. I'll help you."

Your child says: "The duck cried and cried." You say: "Good for you! Was that excellent reading?"

After he answers, you agree or disagree and then move to the next page or have him read this one again.

Occasionally, read the entire book to your child even when he has already figured out how to read it. Also continue to work with him using the highly predictable books. He will feel proud of himself as he discovers that he can figure out how to read these books after minimal interaction with you.

Technique 3: Set an Expectation for Excellence

Just a reminder: don't mislead your child's brain, and don't sugarcoat information. It's OK to occasionally say: "Good try," even if the read was not excellent. But it is better to ask your child to "read it again" or to alternate reading—you read the page, and then your child reads the same page—as many times as it takes for him to read the page excellently. Then you can tell him how smart he is and how proud you are that he is figuring out how to read! He will feel a genuine and well-deserved sense of accomplishment. In addition, remember the following:

- Be ready to help him achieve excellence by using activities to make what he reads more predictable.
- Help him learn to judge his own excellence.
- Create opportunities for him to repeatedly reread books he has mastered (e.g., he can read on his own while you read a newspaper or while older siblings do homework).
- Know how to be an effective coach. Revisit the section by that name (Technique 6 in the Techniques for Using Highly Predictable Books).

Techniques for Introducing Minimal-Print Early Readers

Minimal-print early readers are unpredictable books that do not have a repetitive pattern of language but also do not have a lot of print on each page. Books in this category need to be read aloud to your child more often to increase the predictability of the text. When your child reads them, more coaching from you will be required because the books will be harder for him to predict.

Your child is ready for minimal-print early readers, regardless of his age, when he demonstrates his comfort with and enthusiasm for reading predictable books. When you interact together with minimal print books, use the same activities as those discussed for highly predictable and predictable books.

As your child tries on a subconscious level to make the predictive strategy work, he may change the language in the text more frequently than he did with either the highly predictable or predictable books. Remember that a deviation from the text is an error only if he changes the sentence so that it doesn't make sense, the language is awkward, or what your child reads significantly alters the author's intended message.

Technique 1: Prompts to Use When Errors Occur

The following set of prompts will help you make your child's interactions with minimal-print books more successful:

- If an error occurs as your child is reading, say: "That didn't work. Read it again."
- If necessary, point to the beginning of the sentence so he will know where to begin reading.
- If he keeps making the same error, after you've given the same feedback three times, read the sentence to him and then ask him to read the sentence to you.
- If he continues to change the text in an unacceptable way, say: "You read the sentence like this . . . [read the sentence just as he read it]. But the book says . . . [read the sentence the way it is written]. Read the sentence again."

As you do this, your child will note the differences in how he read and what the text actually says.

A word of caution: whatever you do, do not point out the specific differences to him. He needs to figure this out for himself. It is also important that you *not* use this activity if the changes your child made to the text make sense, sound natural, and don't significantly change the intended meaning. Using this strategy under these circumstances will cause him to become overly focused on individual words rather than the meaning. Changing the text in an appropriate way is a sign that your child is mastering the predictive strategy. It is a sign of strength in reading.

Technique 2: Use the "Stuck" Strategy

As you interact with your child as he reads minimal-print books, you may find that the diminished predictability causes him to sometimes get "stuck." This simply means he cannot make a prediction and go on. As he becomes more sophisticated in using the predictive strategy, he will no longer get stuck. In the meantime, you need an activity to get him "unstuck."

Your job is to make the meaning of the text more predictable so that your child can get unstuck on his own. Your natural tendency will be to help him identify the word at the point at which he is stuck. Don't! Instead, your task is to give him opportunity to implicitly figure out what he should have done to avoid getting stuck in the first place.

Say: "Skip it [the word] and go on." He will continue on, and when he comes to the first punctuation mark after the skipped word or phrase, say: "Now go back to the beginning of the sentence and read it again."

As you say this, if necessary, point to the place in the text where you want him to start again. As he reads the sentence, if he becomes stuck at the same place, give him a couple of meaning-based hints. For example, you can say: "It's an animal that lives in the desert. It has two humps. It can go a long time without water."

The hints need to be given quickly. With experience, you'll get better and better at giving them. If you can't think of any hints, or if the ones you give don't work, tell him the word so he can move on. He doesn't need "think time"—this is not a guessing game.

Always ask your child to reread the sentence on his own with no intervention from you once he is unstuck. If you need to read the sentence to him to help him succeed, do so.

A word of caution: never allow your child to try to figure out a word by sounding it out. His brain needs to remain free to integrate whatever phonetic information it finds useful, from wherever in the word it chooses.

As you provide meaning-based hints to help your child predict, he is free to strategically sample the alphabetic information. He may think, "Hmm. An animal that lives in the desert and starts with the letter *C*," or his brain may receive its most useful information from the *L* at the end of the word!

After all, how many animals can you think of that end with the letter *L*? In the new view of reading, *everything* the brain could possibly use to predict the meaning intended by the author is available as needed.

The stuck strategy allows your child's brain to figure out what information is useful and how to access it. As previously explained, identifying individual words is not what the brain does to make reading happen. The brain strategically samples phonetic information only as required. Don't risk misdirecting the brain by telling it what to do or where to look. When your child becomes unstuck, his brain will have every opportunity to realize implicitly why his predictive strategy was ineffective on the original reading and what it could have done to make it work. When he rereads the sentence, he will have immediate opportunity to employ the strategies that would have prevented him from being stuck in the first place.

Recognizing Progress

If, on a day-to-day basis, you are using these techniques and activities as outlined, and you are keeping the interaction with your child light and fun without imposing expectations for his progress, within three to six months he should begin to show some of the signs of early reading development. In the new view, these are the signs:

- On his own, he regularly chooses reading over other activities.
- He routinely demonstrates that he enjoys spending time independently with the books and audiobooks that you have provided him.
- When he spends time alone with audiobooks, he follows along, turning the pages at the right time.
- When the two of you read together, he enthusiastically participates in anticipating the message.

- He volunteers to read to you from books he has mastered.
- He is eager to "show off" his developing reading ability to the significant people in his life—and maybe even to guests!

Troubleshooting

What if your child is not displaying any of these signs of progress? Then what? Your child may have a different time schedule from the one you would ideally like to see. Reading is complex. He may need more continuous exposure than you anticipate to begin to predict the text, even in highly predictable books. The following techniques may help you discover and remove any blocks.

Technique 1: Relax and Be Patient

It is essential that you not push your child or communicate any kind of anxiety that you may have about his reading development. Doing so may make him doubt his ability to figure it out, create a sense of guilt at your disappointment, contribute to his developing anxiety around reading and a consequent desire to avoid it, or simply cause him to lose interest. The wrong thing to do is inadvertently send him an implicit message that he may be incapable of figuring out the process for himself.

When you are certain you are not communicating any anxiety or disappointment to your child, you can check to see whether he understands these two foundational concepts:

1. There are white spaces between printed words.
2. There is a one-to-one correspondence between reading aloud and words on the page.

Why be concerned about these two concepts now? The answer is that you have already provided your child with plenty of opportunity to develop these important understandings on a subconscious level. If he is not displaying signs of progress in reading development in spite of your consistent and excellent coaching, you need to know whether or not he understands the foundational concepts. The following techniques will help you assess whether he does and help him develop them if he hasn't already done so.

Technique 2: Communicate the Concept of "Printed Words"

Choose a book with just a few words on each page. If your child cannot easily and consistently count at least as high as the number of words on a single page, he is not ready for this interaction. Ask him to count the number of words on one of the pages. If he can do this correctly, then he has an appropriate concept of written words. If he cannot, as evidenced by counting letters instead of words, then this foundational concept needs to be developed.

Explain that you can tell where the words are because of the bigger space separating the words, as compared with the letters. Use the book to point out the bigger spaces between words and to point out how, within a single word, letters are crowded together. Then ask him to count the words again.

- If he starts to count letters rather than words, stop him at the end of the first word. Say: "You did a good job of counting the letters, but I asked you to count words. Remember how we know where the words are?"
- If he can't answer, model counting the words, telling him about the spaces again. Say: "See how these letters are close together and there are big spaces on each end? That's how I know that this is a word [pointing] and this is a word [pointing]. Now I'm going to count the words on this page. Watch me." Count the words, pointing to each as you count.

Move to a new page and ask him to count the words. Coach him through the process if required. Repeat on different pages until he can successfully count the number of words on his own. If he absolutely cannot see that there are spaces between the words, he may have a significant problem with vision or visual perception. Chapter 8 addresses this often overlooked issue.

When your child is consistently successful in counting words, use a sentence with the word *a* or the word *I* in it.

- *If he counts the words correctly*, say: "I tried to fool you because this word [point to it] has only one letter, but you knew it was a word! Aren't you smart!"
- *If he doesn't get it*, say: "Oh, I fooled you. This is a funny word because it has only one letter [point to it], but you can tell it's a word because of these spaces [point to the spaces]."

Give him more sentences containing single-letter words. When he counts the words successfully, say: "Good for you! I can't fool you anymore, can I?"

Once you are certain that your child has the concept of printed words, assess whether or not he has the concept of one-to-one correspondence.

Technique 3: Communicate the Concept of One-to-One Correspondence with Spoken and Printed Words

Gauge your child's understanding of one-to-one correspondence between the written language on the page and the language that is spoken when the page is read. Retrieve one of the highly predictable books with short sentences and read it to your child. Then, have him either read the sentences or interact with you to complete the unpredictable parts. As he reads, pay attention to the amount of language he uses to complete each sentence. If he consistently adds considerably more language than just the few words required or uses only one or a few words where several words are needed, he may have not yet built a concept of one-to-one correspondence. It is an appropriate time to use an extra intervention.

Read a sentence from a highly predictable book out loud to your child, and then ask him to count the words. When he is finished counting, ask him to look at you. As you read the same sentence again, put up a separate finger as each word is pronounced. Then ask him to count the fingers you have raised.

Say: "When I read the sentence, I say the same number of words as there are on the page."

Notice how this language does not call attention to any *single* word. Rather, your goal is to show your child that there is a direct correspondence between the number of words in an author's printed message and the number of words that are read aloud.

Keep in mind that the goal isn't to encourage him to reproduce every word as he reads. Rather, it is to help him realize that there is a relationship between the language spoken during oral reading and the language written on the page. It will be his job to figure out the exact nature of that relationship.

Now go to the next page and read it to your child. Ask him to look at you; as you repeat the sentence, raise one finger each time you pronounce a word. Ask him how many words you said, and let him count your fingers. Once he has completed this, ask him to count the words on the page. Repeat this activity with new pages two or three times until you feel confident he has the right idea.

A word of caution: techniques to build a concept of printed words and one-to-one correspondence between oral reading and print are normally *not* necessary.

Allowing children to develop their own implicit sense of individual words and one-to-one correspondences is best, and most children easily do. However, if your child isn't catching on to the activities outlined for using highly predictable books, ensuring that he has an understanding of words and one-to-one correspondence may be helpful. *Do not* use these two techniques if the activities for using highly predictable books are working, and never repeat them. Overdoing it may send an erroneous message that you want your child to focus on the words as he reads.

Once you are certain that your child has the concepts of printed words and one-to-one correspondence, if he still isn't making progress, you should do an honest appraisal of your coaching skills.

Technique 4: Evaluate Yourself

Self-checks are important. It is possible that you may not be implementing the techniques and activities in a smooth, seamless, and efficient manner, causing your child to feel uncomfortable with the activities, or some outside influence may be interfering with your coaching. Make sure you are doing all of the activities appropriately and in a manner that is enjoyable to your child. Make sure no one else—babysitters, day-care providers, relatives, preschool teachers, and so on—is focusing your child's attention on individual words during reading activities. In addition, make sure you are not putting undue pressure on him that is causing him to worry about disappointing you.

When you are certain that you are coaching appropriately and your child is still not displaying signs of progress, two possibilities remain: he is not yet interested in figuring out the reading process or there is an authentic barrier to reading development.

Technique 5: What to Do if Your Child Is Not Yet Interested in Figuring Out the Reading Process

If your child shows insufficient interest, keep reading to him, including from highly predictable books, and occasionally try out some of the activities. Treat this casually; don't let him feel that he is failing—*he isn't*. Continue to make it fun. His brain just doesn't want to work on it right now. It's probably busily figuring out something else. Don't forget that it is possible to undermine your child's intent or, worse, send him signals that he is a failure if you try to push him when he is neither interested nor ready.

Technique 6: What to Do if Your Child Has an Authentic Barrier to Reading Development

The more common barriers to reading development are an implicit belief that reading is about decoding and the identification of words, the lack of sufficient language skills, a problem with visual processing that interferes with intent and attention, problems in coordinating the integrated process of passage reading, and brain defects. In most cases, these issues can be successfully addressed in the new view of reading and reading development. To explore these possibilities in more detail, see Chapter 8.

Lists of Books Representing Each of the Six Categories

In the Appendix, you will find a collection of books that has been used by the READ RIGHT company for years to help children learn to read and to help struggling readers eliminate their reading problems. It is divided into the six important categories discussed. As soon as you locate some of these books (through libraries, bookstores, or online book services) and become familiar with the characteristics of each category, you will be prepared to locate other books that share the same characteristics.

Sets of books for each category also are available for purchase through the READ RIGHT company. Inquiries must come through e-mail to info@readright.com. We continuously add books to our lists.

For the Child Who Thinks Simple Books Are "Too Easy"

Occasionally, I encounter children who feel that the simple books included in the book lists are "too easy." The daughter of a friend of mine offers a perfect example. As I spoke with my friend about how he might encourage his five-year-old to begin the process of figuring out reading, I showed him a few highly predictable books. His reaction: "Oh, my child won't be interested in these books. They're much too simple. I'm reading the Harry Potter books to her at bedtime, and she loves them. She won't like these."

My friend has a point. I suggested that he ask his daughter if she wants to learn to read. If she says, "Yes!" then I suggested that he tell her that together they would read some books that might help her. This established a different purpose for the activity, thereby preparing her for the simpler highly predictable books. She wasn't set up to "judge" the early readers based on interest. Instead, she was prepared to become highly engaged in the activity of figuring out the complex process of passage reading.

Do not use this strategy with your child unless he has provided you with a significant reason to suspect that he will reject the early readers. For example, he has said to you: "I don't like that book. It's not exciting." Rather, introduce the highly predictable books, predictable books, and books with minimal print without telling your child the purpose. You don't want him to know that he's engaged in activities that you think might help him figure out how to read. It isn't necessary; in fact, it isn't even desirable. It is more desirable for him to want to figure out the passage-reading process on his own because *he* sees value in it. If he enjoys the early readers, you never have to share the purpose.

PART III
Challenges to Reading Development

This section focuses on the challenges that can arise as parents and educators seek to create a solid foundation for children's reading development. What are the issues that have the potential to prevent children from constructing excellent reading ability? Are there early warning signs of a reading problem in the making? How might parents and educators unintentionally impede reading development? You will find answers to all three of these questions in the following chapters.

8

Identifying and Overcoming Authentic Barriers to Reading Development

In 1999, authors Susan Hall and Louisa Moats cited four causes of reading problems: (1) word recognition difficulties, (2) the inability to break words down to their discrete sounds (phonemes), (3) difficulty with fluency and comprehension because of the inability to quickly and accurately identify words, and (4) a genetic condition. Note that three out of these four proposed barriers to effective reading relate directly to the same thing—the inability to identify words.

In the interactive constructivist view, the barriers to developing excellent reading ability are very different. They have little to do with the ability to identify words and everything to do with how we first learn to read. You have already seen in Chapter 3 that all knowledge you acquire and construct becomes encoded in the brain in such a way that the physical structure looks almost like a dense jungle of vines and branches. Because of this, it seems appropriate to use a metaphor of being lost in a jungle to consider reading's true barriers.

A child—a daughter, in these examples—could become lost for several reasons. First, perhaps she is focused on a path that will not take her out of the jungle. A second possibility is that none of the available paths leads out of the jungle, and the child hasn't yet figured out that she will have to blaze her own trail. Third, perhaps she is tired of trying to find her way out and simply gives up. Fourth, there may be things in the jungle that continually confuse her and cause her to do the wrong things in the process of choosing a path. And finally, she may be injured and thereby incapable of finding her way out.

In the interactive constructivist view, the barriers to reading development are similar to the five suggested circumstances that might keep a child lost in a jungle:

1. Faulty guidance or instruction that has caused the child to focus on word identification as the main event of reading. (The child is focused on a path that will not take her out of the jungle.)
2. Failure to recognize that the only path to excellent reading ability is to establish an appropriate concept of what is required to read with excellence and to work toward that standard until it is met. (None of the available paths leads out of the jungle, and the child hasn't yet figured out that she will have to blaze her own trail.)
3. Lack of sufficient intent to experiment with figuring out the reading process, eventually leading to abandonment. (She may be tired of trying to find her way out and may simply have given up.)
4. Significant processing disturbances that impede the brain from easily and comfortably interpreting information or that impair the ability to switch between neural networks. (There may be things in the jungle that continually confuse her and cause her to do the wrong things in the process of choosing a path.)
5. Significant brain damage, deficit, or deformity that impairs brain function. (The child is lost in the jungle because she is injured and thereby incapable of finding her way out.)

These potential causes of reading problems are quite different from simply being unable to identify words, aren't they? Consider each one separately.

The Primary Cause of Reading Problems: Focus on the Identification of Words

Let's return to the metaphor of the jungle. Picture a girl who becomes fixated on one particular tree way in the distance. She is so focused on the tree that she fails to see paths to the left or right of her! Rather than explore the other paths, the child remains steadfastly focused on the one that takes her straight to the tree of interest. In the process, she walks right past all of the other paths, not even realizing they are there.

Metaphorically, this is what happens if a child remains focused on individual word identification as the main event of passage reading. She *cannot* find the path to excellent reading if her attention remains only on decoding or any other strategy that keeps her focused primarily on the identification of words.

Granted, many people figure out the process of reading even though at one time or another they were directed to decode words, but it is only because these individuals' brains implicitly stumbled onto a different path—they *experimented* with other ways to use the collection of symbols on a page. Being the marvel of efficiency that it is, the subconscious brain is capable of "looking away" from the tree of interest for a time and exploring other paths. The child who chooses to engage in this kind of implicit experimentation has the opportunity to make new and valuable discoveries about more efficient and effective ways to read.

If at any time your child begins to sound out words or point to words, this is cause for immediate action. Pointing is almost always a learned behavior and an indicator that your child is focused on each individual word. Her brain needs to be free to make its own decisions about where to look to strategically sample the print in its quest to anticipate the author's message. If you see any indication that your child does not have her full attention on the author's meaning, it is imperative that you increase the amount of time you spend with the activities described in Chapters 4 through 7.

As you engage her in the activities, whenever she attempts to decode or points to a word, redirect her focus away from word identification and back to meaning. For example:

- "Read the sentence again, and this time, don't sound out the words. Think about what the sentence is saying."
- "Don't sound out the words. Read it again so that you feel more comfortable."
- "Never point to the words, even if your teacher tells you to. It will slow you down. You can read wonderfully without pointing." (Encourage her to have her teacher talk to you if this creates a problem.)
- "Relax and enjoy the story. Don't worry about the words. Just tell me what's happening on this page."

Be aware that when your child starts school, she is almost guaranteed to be engaged in activities designed to help her brain figure out how to identify words through decoding, word attack, and sight-word strategies. As she enters this environment, it is vital that you continue the activities described in this book to ensure that she keeps on the right path. More on this is discussed in Chapter 9.

Inability to Establish an Appropriate Concept of Excellent Reading

Think about this for a moment: knowing what you know about yourself, how long do you think you would wander in a jungle before you decided that what you were doing wasn't working? Five minutes? An hour? A day? I am convinced there are children (and adults) who would spend their entire lives wandering unsuccessfully rather than experiment with new ways to solve the reading puzzle. Sadly, they come to believe they can't solve it, so they cease to look for a better way.

I, myself, wasted too much time trying to figure out how to use accepted theories and existing methodologies to help my own son with his reading problem. For months, the capable teachers at my son's school and I were locked into a repetitive cycle of trying the same old things that didn't work. It wasn't until my brain connected a seemingly unrelated event to my son's situation that I finally figured out that there had to be a better way to address his reading problem. Remember the event? It was the day my friend's car broke down for the umpteenth time and she declared, "There has to be a mechanic out there who knows how to fix my car!"

Well, there wasn't a "mechanic" out there who knew how to fix my son's reading problem. However, I was convinced the knowledge existed, but I would have to find it. I realize now that, in that moment, I rejected the standard of excellence set for reading instruction by popular reading theorists and went in search of a brand-new standard of excellence.

The search for excellence supports the development of *any* kind of ability. Likewise, settling for *less* than excellence (which often means settling for the status quo) can impede the development of any kind of ability. The minute we are satisfied that something is "good enough," our path is set. We do not move away from "good enough" to something better until we decide that the path we are on simply *isn't* "good enough." In the absence of a serious physical defect, anyone who is lost in any kind of metaphorical jungle is lost in part because the person has not figured out that he or she has to blaze the trail. People have to construct success for themselves, and this usually means doing things in a way that they have never been done before.

What can cause your child to fail to establish an appropriate concept of what it is to read with excellence? Here are three ways it can happen:

- If you tell her that she read excellently when she didn't
- If you praise every attempt at reading, whether excellence was produced or not
- If you ignore nonexcellent reads as if they didn't happen

To understand excellent reading on the most important level, below the level of consciousness, developing readers must *experience it.* If you follow the techniques in Chapter 7, your child will experience excellent reading for herself. Then, if you consistently encourage her to hold herself to the standard of excellence, her marvelous brain will come to settle for no less than the production of excellence every time she reads.

Lack of Strong Intent

Who or what is in charge of your intentions? Is the conscious "you" in charge? Or, is it the subconscious "you"? This is a large and important question. Most of us like to think that we are consciously in charge of everything we do, but the reality is that there are aspects of who we are that are guided below our own level of consciousness. We can possess surface-level intent, but it is the subconscious intent that truly is in the driver's seat.

Subconscious intent is a powerful force in the mind of every individual. Specific behaviors can help you identify whether low intent is contributing to a child's struggle with reading. A child with low intent will show one or more of these signs:

- She resists engaging in what you ask her to do.
- She verbalizes disagreement or skepticism or argues with you.
- She isn't enthusiastic when she works with you.
- She wants to direct the activity even though she isn't able to do it.
- She absolutely refuses to "look and learn."

Intent is a powerful force of nature—a *mental force*. Through intent, humankind has built pyramids, gone to the moon, and overcome tremendous adversity. In the interactive constructivist view, intent is literally the fuel that drives learning.

If your child displays low intent, first, consider whether you may be imposing on her your desire for her to be an early reader and, as a result, communicating disappointment if she isn't meeting your time schedule. Second, if you are not imposing your desires on her, evaluate whether you are following the techniques in Chapter 5 appropriately. Either way, ease up on the techniques described in Chapters 6 and 7 and increase the amount of activities detailed in Chapter 5 until she begins to exhibit sufficient interest and intent.

Processing Disturbances and "Switching" Problems

The brain must be able to process auditory and visual information appropriately in order to make sense of the world, and the brain must be able to plan, control, and coordinate neural activity in a manner that easily accesses and makes sense of information. Both sensory processing and appropriate "switching" between neural systems are necessary for excellent reading.

Auditory Processing

Currently, some popular reading theorists believe that difficulty in auditory processing—problems hearing the sounds of speech—can cause reading problems. In addition, a number of reading theorists have declared that *explicit awareness* of how we string discrete sounds together to form words when we talk is a foundational concept for reading development. These theorists suggest that an absence of what they call phonemic awareness is an important cause of reading failure.

If this were true, how could any deaf child learn to read? *The child couldn't.* Also, if a hearing child didn't know on an implicit level that discrete sounds must be strung together to enable talking, wouldn't it show up in the child's speech? Further, if the child couldn't effectively process the sounds of speech, how could that child learn to pronounce words correctly?

In the READ RIGHT® company's experience dealing with thousands of adults and children who struggle with reading, we rarely find anyone who also struggles to pronounce words. The vast majority of struggling readers are excellent talkers, pronouncing every word correctly.

In the interactive constructivist view, if your child can comfortably express her thinking through talking, she possesses all the implicit knowledge of language she needs in order to be able to learn to read—including knowledge of the sounds of speech. All she needs to do to be prepared for reading is to learn the association between particular sounds of language and the letters of the alphabet that represent those sounds (not *all* of the letters of the alphabet, only the "stable" letters; see Chapter 6). You can relax and not worry about "auditory processing problems" or "phonemic awareness deficits."

What if your child cannot pronounce particular sounds of speech correctly? When this happens, it typically involves only one or two sounds. In extreme cases, mispronunciation may involve more sounds and result in a lack of clarity that makes it difficult for the child to be understood. In either case, there is still no reason to panic about her reading potential. We read with our eyes, not with our ears. The brain doesn't decode to read with excellence. It goes directly to the meaning by anticipating the author's message.

Possible Signs of Auditory or Language Processing Problems. If your child can't articulate all the sounds of speech in a standard way, or if she seems to have trouble expressing her thinking through talking, then she may have problems with auditory processing or language processing. Watch for these signs:

- She may not speak clearly.
- She may not be able to pronounce certain sounds of speech.
- She may be confused about spoken language.
- She may struggle to organize spoken language.
- She may be irritated by loud sounds, as evidenced by complaints and/or covering or plugging her ears, indicating problems with volume control (the amount of and/or the type of sound).

Helping a Child with Auditory or Language Processing Problems. Only a qualified professional can properly identify these issues. You may choose to consult a speech and language professional for guidance in helping your child pronounce speech sounds in a standard way or helping resolve any confusion about language. Unaddressed speech or language problems could cause social embarrassment and, in extreme cases, avoidance of talking. In the interactive constructivist view, however, lack of clarity in speech does not directly contribute to a reading problem.

With an older child, a speech therapist might choose to use flash cards with words on them as a vehicle to address pronunciation issues. Be aware that, if this is done, such focus on individual printed words can contribute to an implicit belief by your child that focusing on words is what one does to read, thereby laying the foundation for a reading problem. Simply ask the speech therapist to avoid any activities associated with your child's identifying individual words from flash cards or word lists.

Is there anything you can do at home to head off the potential for language-related problems? Yes! You can make sure that you have created an environment in which your child is consistently surrounded with meaningful spoken language and is expected to respond with her own meaningful language.

Visual Processing

The other sensory system that has a potential impact on reading ability is the visual processing system. This may seem obvious, but surprisingly, many reading experts and medical doctors dismiss the potential for difficulties with this system to contribute to reading problems. The fallacy of this position has been challenged.

Everyone would agree that you have to be able to see the print on the page well enough to make reading possible. This, however, is not a statement about visual processing. It is a statement about *visual acuity*—the ability to see letters on an eye chart. Acuity issues are dealt with by ophthalmologists (medical doctors) and optometrists through conventional glasses for nearsightedness, farsightedness, and astigmatism. But what about visual processing issues? They are far more complex because they have little to do with the mechanics of the eye. Rather, they involve the deep structures of the brain and have to do with what we perceive (perception) and our thought processes (cognition). For example, visual processing problems might involve print that does not appear stable or might involve excess or inappropriate brain activity that makes control over visual perception difficult. Visual processing problems cannot be addressed with conventional glasses.

In the interactive constructivist view, visual processing issues do not *cause* reading problems. Instead, they *contribute* to reading problems in a rather insidious way. When a child struggles to gain control over her own visual perception, sometimes experiencing eyestrain, headaches, or fatigue as she expends tremendous energy in an effort to maintain control over inappropriate activity in her brain, she appears to fall behind her peers in classroom reading activities. The teacher assumes she is having difficulty with the cognitive aspects of reading, such as decoding skills, and tells the child to focus more closely on the words. As the problem persists, the teacher makes arrangements for the child to get extra "help" in the form of additional phonics, decoding, and/or sight-word instruction. See the dilemma? The actual issue was a processing problem, but the intervention designed to catch the child up causes her to focus more directly on the identification of individual words! As her focus on word identification increases, it becomes less and less likely that she will experiment with other strategies in her quest to figure out the passage-reading process. In a more appropriate instructional environment, her brain would be directed to figure out how to develop appropriate strategies for sampling alphabetic information *in spite of* the visual processing problem. Instead, she is continuously refocused on words.

These children end up with a double deficit—the unidentified visual processing problem and increased, more intense instruction that causes the brain to focus on the *wrong activities* while constructing neural circuitry to guide reading.

Possible Signs of a Visual Processing Problem. In some but not all cases, it is possible to spot a child with a visual processing problem. Look for one or more of the following indicators:

• She may complain about print "moving" and not being able to see clearly, but her tests with eye charts show no problem.
• She may resist close work.
• She may be unusually clumsy or have extreme difficulty catching balls, signaling problems with depth perception.
• She may be confused about things that she sees and have unusual difficulty with "hidden picture" activities.
• She may frequently do one or more of the following when working with books and other close work: (1) place her hands over her eyes to shade them, (2) cover one eye to see, (3) purposefully tilt her head, (4) rub her eyes a lot, or (5) struggle with fatigue.

Helping a Child with a Visual Processing Problem. What should parents do if they see any of these signs? A thorough functional vision examination should be mandatory for every child who has any of the possible signs of a visual processing problem. Though rare, issues with vision can be related to a serious health problem, too. Her pediatrician can rule this out.

But here is where things become complicated. Opinions on the topic of visual processing issues are diverse. There is considerable disagreement among individuals and even among professional groups. Associations that represent ophthalmologists—the medical doctors of the eye—do not believe visual processing problems are relevant to learning or to reading development. They have issued controversial opinion statements advising consumers not to be taken in by what they regard as questionable practices to screen for and treat visual processing issues. Keep in mind that these doctors specialize in the mechanics of the eye, not in the deep structures of the brain, where visual processing problems manifest.

Many optometrists, too, are skeptical about the existence of visual processing problems and will not provide screening beyond the standard eye exam. However, a small group of behavioral optometrists who are certified to perform developmental vision therapy acknowledge the importance of visual processing issues and test for and treat them. But vision therapy can be costly, and the evidence and opinions as to its effectiveness are mixed.

A small group of psychologists and educators believe that some children's visual systems are overly sensitive to certain lighting conditions, often including fluorescent light typically found in the classroom. This condition, called *Irlen syndrome* or *scotopic sensitivity syndrome*, creates problems for those affected by making it difficult for them to process visual information if the lighting is not compatible with their visual systems. Evidence and opinions about this syndrome are also mixed, and treatment can be expensive.

All of these groups embrace their own views and have taken critical stands against one another as to the validity of the underlying problems, the methods of diagnoses, and recommended treatments. Frankly, the situation is a mess, leaving children to sit in classrooms trying to cope with visual processing problems and often getting little or no assistance from the medical, vision, or education communities.

If you seek screening for visual processing problems, request assessment that focuses on a child's ability to perform close-up work with comfort and ease under lighting conditions typical of the classroom. Conventional vision exams often occur in dimly lit rooms and involve artificial test instruments that have little relationship with the kind of near work that children are asked to perform in classrooms.

Until scientists sort out the role of visual processing in learning and reading development, what can you do? First, be alert. Watch for the signs of a visual processing problem as your child begins to learn to read, *but don't worry about it!* In my company's experience with struggling readers, seldom do visual processing problems prevent people from becoming excellent readers when their brains are compelled to do the right things for reading. It may delay the process to some degree and be the source of physical discomfort (eyestrain, fatigue, and headaches), but these students can still become excellent readers.

Activities to Support Your Child's Healthy Visual System. If you want to assist your young child in developing a healthy visual system, common sense says the child should be routinely engaged in activities requiring complex visual work. Activities such as watching television or videos do not involve complex processing because they are passive and do not require your child to fixate on an isolated area of the television screen. Activities that *do* involve complex visual processing include the following:

- Focusing on print (your child follows along with you while you read aloud, and she begins to make attempts at reading)
- Doing puzzles and art projects that require highly specific fixation
- Any other activities you can think of that cause your child to stretch her span of recognition (how much information her brain perceives during a fixation)

Your child may benefit most from early opportunities to work with black print on white pages. Black print on white paper can be stressful to the visual system because it requires a broader span of recognition and involves a great deal of straight lines, curves, and a high degree of contrast, all of which make visual processing more complex. If vision is indeed adaptive, as the upside-down vision experiments described in Chapter 1 suggest, then it stands to reason that it would be beneficial from an early age for children to have opportunities to be consistently exposed to complex visual work. A brain that has mastered complex visual work is ready to effectively sample alphabetic information.

Great examples of activities that might help to support both span of recognition and adaptation of the visual system to black-on-white print are the "Hidden Pictures" activities in *Highlights for Children* magazines. Children tend to love this magazine and enjoy finding the objects hidden in the simple drawings. At first, you and your child can have fun doing the activities together, and once your child gets the idea, she can take over on her own. Other activities great for this kind of visual development are mazes, dot-to-dot activities, and incomplete pictures in which children fill in the missing lines.

Like other educators and professionals who work with children, I am eager to see more research on visual processing issues and associated interventions. So long as the interventions and therapies do not involve *any form* of reading instruction, they should not interfere with your child's reading development. Any intervention that could increase a child's comfort while reading is worthy of consideration, especially if increased comfort leads to greater willingness to spend time with books.

Efficient and Effective "Switching"

Separate from sensory processing issues, there is evidence that some children may struggle with "switching" among neural networks in the brain. For passage reading, executive functions must direct the brain in anticipating or predicting how to integrate all of the activity that must occur to achieve comprehension of an author's intended message. This complex activity occurs below the level of consciousness.

Researchers working in the field of mathematics recently identified problems with cognitive switching among children with learning difficulties. R. Bull and G. Scerif found that the primary difficulty for struggling math students was switching from an old strategy to a new one, implying inefficiency in executive functioning.

In the interactive constructivist view of reading development, problems associated with executive functioning are automatically addressed when the brain is held to a high standard of excellence in reading. The brain has to correct its own problems with "switching" in order to read efficiently. It can overcome the problem by applying mental force to the challenge.

Brain Damage, Deficit, or Deformity

Fortunately, the number of children born with structurally different brains that are incapable of functioning in a normal way is small. Impairment can be mild to severe, but, in the interactive constructivist view, only children who are so severely impaired that they struggle to function at all are prevented from becoming functional readers.

Dyslexia is the most common disorder for which a structural brain difference is offered as an explanation for the existence of a severe reading problem. Of the twenty thousand people with whom we have worked, it is impossible to know how many might have been clinically diagnosed as "dyslexic." The clinical diagnosis typically is made by professionals trained in the fields of medicine or psychology, and few families tend to pursue the diagnosis, because of the expense or the negative label it assigns to children. The majority of families leave it to schools to help their children overcome reading problems.

The International Dyslexia Association (IDA) defines dyslexia as a "specific learning disability that is neurological in origin." Individuals with dyslexia, the IDA claims, struggle with accurate or fluent word recognition, spelling, and decoding, with the difficulties typically resulting from "a deficit in the phonological component of language"—or, difficulty with the ability to distinguish the sounds of oral speech. The IDA's definition clearly buys into the belief that most reading problems are associated with lack of ability in decoding and word-identification skills.

The belief that reading is all about individual words has been fueled in recent years by studies designed specifically to measure what happens in the brain when test subjects identify individual words from lists. In the interactive constructivist view, such information is interesting but not relevant because word identification and passage reading are not seen as the same cognitive acts. The studies conclude that poor readers register less neural activation than good readers in a few specific language areas of the brain. Such research has concluded that poor readers have trouble decoding and so can't create a neural replica of a word in a proposed "word form" area of the brain, making reading difficult.

Newer brain studies verify that identifying words from lists and reading passages of text involve significantly *different activity* in the brain. One study has even shown that the *same neural activation pattern* is registered when subjects identify objects in a room *or* pictures of objects *or* sounds in a room *or* words from a list. The researchers concluded that the brain regions involved were performing a naming function, rather than performing a decoding and word-storage function.

Remember Jordan, whom you met in Chapter 3? Jordan may have structural problems with the speech centers of his brain, but he didn't need to fix his speech problem in order to fix his reading problem. Actually, it was quite the opposite.

Fixing his reading problem has helped his ability to speak and his ability to verbally express his thinking.

Even though Ken Reinertsen, introduced in Chapter 6, didn't have a speech problem, he was as a teen diagnosed with severe dyslexia at a prestigious clinic. In his adult years, he did what he was not supposed to be able to do. He completely eliminated his reading problem—and he did it with methodology that ignores the idea that dyslexia is caused by so-called phonological processing deficits. His success and the success of others like him are a clear indicator that phonological processing issues become moot when the brain is compelled to do the right things with reading.

Help for Older Readers

If you suspect an older child has a reading problem, you can determine if your suspicion is accurate. Listen to her read out loud from books appropriate to her grade level and assess whether she is doing the process absolutely correctly by answering these questions:

- Does the child sound totally natural? She must be able to read seamlessly every time, with no unnatural pauses, not even slight ones.
- Does she have to reread text to understand it even when she agrees that the content is not complex? Excellent readers do not need to read text over again. They construct the meaning as they go and, in the process, comprehend everything as it is read.
- Do you feel a total sense of comfort while you listen to her read, and do you sense that she, too, is totally comfortable? Excellent readers don't have to "work" to make reading happen. The process is as effortless as talking.
- Without suggestion from anyone, does she choose to read as a free-time activity? If she avoids reading, it may be a

sign that she is experiencing a mild to severe struggle with reading.

It is far easier to guide a child into excellent reading ability in the first place than to "fix" a reading problem after it has been "soft-wired" into the brain. A child who has a reading problem has built a neural network that fails to guide the reading process appropriately. To eliminate the problem, the brain must be compelled to remodel the existing network so that it produces excellent reading. The brain will be highly resistive to performing the remodeling work, but it can be compelled to do so if the environment is right.

What kind of environment is required? The necessary environment is one that causes the brain to establish an appropriate concept of excellence, develop and maintain strong intent, and engage in an implicit predictive strategy involving a series of experiments on the journey to making new discoveries about how to make excellent reading happen. Sound familiar? Yes, it probably isn't surprising to you that the same elements discussed throughout this book are required. However, the brain of the struggling reader won't be as receptive because it has *already built* neural circuitry to guide reading. Remember, even though brains are highly "plastic," they are resistive to change!

A significant amount of training is required to be able to intervene appropriately with a struggling reader. Tutors at centers and schools using the READ RIGHT intervention program to address reading problems undergo seven weeks of intensive hands-on training and monitoring during the first year. It would be impossible to convey all of the information associated with that training here. Additionally, just getting your child to cooperate can be difficult. Most children with reading problems do not relish the thought of "another reading program." They have been through too many that have not worked for them. Nevertheless, there are some things that you can try.

First, encourage your child. Help her remain positive about her reading potential. Let her know that you will do everything you can to help and support her and that you believe in her ability to figure out the reading process. She *must* maintain hope so she will have the strong intent needed to continue to experiment with reading.

Second, continue to read with her regularly, and do your best to follow the techniques and activities offered in Chapter 7. Treat the situation almost as though you are starting with reading from scratch. Read this book again, and follow the activities faithfully and correctly. Do not vary in any way that would cause your child to focus on the wrong things, such as individual words! Remember that you need to start with highly predictable books and hold your child strictly accountable to produce excellent reading every time she reads. Once she can read both predictable and minimal-print books with excellence, gradually introduce books that have slightly longer sentences and slightly longer paragraphs. Continue advancing to increasingly complex text as your child demonstrates her ability to read with excellence from the current level of text. Be sure to continue using the techniques outlined in Chapter 7.

Third, remember that the human brain—while resistive to change—is a remarkable learning machine. If learning isn't occurring, the problem is almost never the *child*. Rather, the culprit is almost always inappropriate instruction.

Finding a Program Based in the Interactive Constructivist View

If the preceding approaches don't work, see if you can find a reading intervention program with a strong base in the interactive constructivist view. The characteristics of such a program would include the following:

- The program recognizes that all process learning (including reading) operates primarily implicitly and so cannot be explicitly taught.
- A constructivist program does not rely on work sheets, workbooks, or software programs; instructional materials

do not cause the brain to remodel the neural circuitry that guides reading.

• A constructivist program recognizes that a child must figure out reading for herself and creates an environment that compels her brain to get the work done.

READ RIGHT is such a constructivist reading program; others may exist. You might find one, and if you do, *please* let me know! I'd love to welcome another program to the interactive constructivist family.

Finally, if your concern about your child's reading ability is turning into anxiety, consider having your child tutored long-distance through telephone by a certified READ RIGHT tutor. Several years ago, we were able to successfully adapt the program to a long-distance learning model. The only significant difference between READ RIGHT delivered by telephone and the program being delivered in person is the face-to-face contact that in-person tutoring involves. Nearly everything else about the program remains the same. For more information, inquire on the Internet at readright.com or call (360) 427-9440. Costs are similar to those associated with other nationally implemented tutoring programs. The program is guaranteed. If you are not satisfied with the results after eight sessions and all tutoring materials are returned, you will receive a refund.

Success Story: Light Sensitivity and Dyslexia

Light sensitivity may have played a role in the early reading failure of Tom, another of our clients diagnosed with severe dyslexia.

In the second grade, Tom was evaluated for learning disabilities at Children's Hospital of Boston. Clinicians there noted significant gaps between his cognitive ability and his performance. According to his mother, they communicated that he could not be expected to do well academically. Tom's mother found the news rather chilling: he would be able to learn only basic living skills.

In fourth grade, Tom began spending most of his school day in a resource room with special education interventions. For grades seven and eight, he attended a renowned residential school for dyslexic students. In grade ten, he attended a public school and was provided with remedial instruction through a popular and highly regarded reading method. Despite all of these interventions, Tom graduated from high school reading at a second-grade level.

When Tom was twenty-three, he began long-distance telephone tutoring with READ RIGHT methodology. He participated in twice-weekly, hour-long tutoring sessions by phone and, in slightly more than two hundred hours, eliminated his reading problem. In his mid-twenties, Tom enrolled in college.

In March 2003, Tom's mother reported that he had earned a 4.0 in his winter quarter of college. Additionally, Tom had taken courses for national emergency medical technician certification and passed the required exams on the first try. Some of Tom's study partners, who had not experienced learning disabilities as children or teens, failed the exam on the first attempt. Tom maintained a 3.3 GPA throughout college. In December 2003, at the end of his junior year, he made a personal decision to leave college and start his own business. In preparation, he read a plethora of business-oriented books.

In interviews before he left college, Tom confided that his reading speed was still slower than he would like; he also reported that certain lighting conditions (usually poor-quality fluorescent lights) interfered with his physical comfort and visual stability in college classrooms.

If, indeed, Tom is sensitive to certain types of fluorescent light, he may well have been one of those children who struggle in classrooms every year because lighting conditions are a poor match with their visual systems. For years, adults have complained about lighting conditions in offices and department stores, yet little concern has been expressed for what this may mean for young children with overly sensitive visual systems. It is an issue that needs more attention by the scientific community.

9

When Paths Diverge: Your Child Goes to School

Some time ago, a business acquaintance asked for advice in dealing with his six-year-old son, David. Divorced, Fred saw his son regularly on alternate weekends and for a month during the summer. He explained that he had read to David from an early age and that both had always enjoyed their time with books. However, when David started kindergarten, things began to change. Both his kindergarten teacher and his maternal grandmother, a retired first-grade teacher, began working with David to help him develop early reading skills. Their focus was on teaching phonics and then instructing David to use that knowledge to sound out words. David wasn't very good at performing the associated tasks, and by the time he started first grade, he was already well behind his peers in reading. David's parents, of course, were concerned, as was his grandmother. All redoubled their efforts, and Fred made a commitment to work diligently with David whenever they were together.

David continued to fall behind. Troubled, Fred told us: "Now David refuses to try to read to me, and he won't even let me read to him! We used to enjoy our time together with books. Not anymore. David starts tearing up, ready to cry, if he even sees me with a book."

I explained to Fred that the consistent and focused effort on sounding out words probably was causing David's severe reading problem. The challenge would be to encourage David's brain to experiment implicitly with new strategies to figure out the reading process. I volunteered to train Fred to work with his son.

When David arrived to spend a month between first and second grades with his father, the three of us met for training sessions in the techniques that are now presented in this book. David was reluctant to work with me or his father. But it didn't take many sessions to win him over. Soon, he was comfortably interacting with the highly predictable books, and he actually seemed to enjoy it. After a few hands-on lessons from me, Fred took over with his son. Other family members were impressed with David's improvement, and they began to follow the techniques, too. By the end of second grade, David no longer had a reading problem. He read better than most of his peers. His dad, with pride and a twinkle in his eye, said: "We've created a monster! David always has his nose in a book, and at bedtime, he's always begging me to let him read 'just one more'."

David was obviously capable of learning how to read with excellence, so why did he have so much trouble? The answer is likely obvious by now: he had been taught by well-meaning adults to decode and identify each and every word. The brain does what you tell it to do; therefore, telling it to do the right thing is essential.

Telling the Brain to Do the Right Thing

If you have followed the techniques in this book consistently and faithfully, you have been telling your child's brain to do the right thing with reading, and you are seeing the evidence of your success in your child's performance. Depending on how much knowledge of language your child has and how long you have been engaging him or her in the activities, your child will be well on the road to becoming an excellent reader. You can know that the latter is the case if you see these characteristics:

- Your child is responding enthusiastically to the activities outlined in this book.
- Your child no longer needs highly predictable books because he is learning to draw upon his own knowledge to make accurate predictions and has begun to anticipate the author's intended message successfully with less predictable books.
- When your child "reads" to you, it almost always sounds natural.
- Your child chooses to read—sometimes to himself.

A teacher probably won't be able to "see" your child's progress the way you can because the teacher's evaluation criteria are rooted in a set of assumptions that are different from yours. A teacher will want to know if students can identify individual words—probably initially from word lists rather than in stories—and won't be impressed if students can read only text they have already heard and seen many times. Why? Because the teacher believes the main event of reading is identifying words and won't understand the importance of getting the brain to anticipate the author's message. If your child has not yet figured out the complex, implicit act of passage reading well enough to perform with excellence in reading unfamiliar text, a teacher simply may not recognize the progress your child has made toward that goal.

The idea of developing a concept of excellence for passage reading as the important first step in reading development is not on the radar screens of educators. They tend to believe that the correct identification of each and every word is more important than the production of reading that always—even from the very beginning—makes sense, feels comfortable to the reader, and seems like conversational speech.

Giving Mixed Messages to the Brain

If your child already is a reader by the time he enters kindergarten or first grade, celebrate! Excellent readers remain excellent readers for life. Exposure to the inaccurate messages designed to cause them to focus on individual words will not have an ill effect. Their brains know better! However, if your child is not yet an excellent reader, such exposure to decoding and word-identification strategies has the potential to impede the experimenting that your child has begun to do to figure out the reading process.

What are the signals that your child is being adversely affected by mixed messages concerning what the brain must do to read? Primarily, they comprise any reading behavior that indicates that your child is beginning to use word-identification strategies. For example:

- Explicit "sounding out" of words
- Pointing at words while reading
- Using a card to block part of the text from view (frequently encouraged by teachers to prevent losing the place as the reader moves from one line of text to the next)
- Spelling out words prior to reading them
- Beginning to sound less natural while working with books—an indication that the child's brain is experimenting with word-identification strategies

Ideally, a classroom teacher would not send messages to your child's brain that present word identification as the main event of the reading process, but given the widespread acceptance of that assumption by the reading field and the lay public, that ideal is unlikely. You may be able to influence the teacher's thinking—or at least make the teacher aware that you have chosen to engage your child in another view of reading and reading development. The tips in the following sections may be helpful.

Talk to Your Child's Teacher

As soon as your child starts any kind of school—preschool, kindergarten, or first grade—find out what kind of reading instruction your child will be exposed to. Today, most early classroom instruction focuses on phonics, decoding skills, and individual word recognition in the early grades and often in the later grades, as well, for students who are displaying reading problems. State and federal governments are heavily supporting these programs at the moment (the pendulum has shifted several times throughout history), and, all too often now, teachers are required by law or district policy to use a specific curriculum. As soon as possible, let your child's teacher know that you have chosen to introduce your child to reading through a new view that makes a lot of sense to you, and invite the teacher to read this book. If the teacher declines, it is important to respect that decision. If the teacher does agree to read it, ask if the two of you can discuss the book after he or she finishes it. This will give you an opportunity to share with the teacher your experiences in using the activities at home with your child.

Use Supporting Information to Address Resistance

Periodically visit our website at readright.com. Download any information that you think could be of interest to your child's teacher and share it with him or her. Suggest that the teacher call our office to get a list of references. We can put the teacher in direct contact with other teachers, school administrators, students, and parents all across the country who use the methodology. Good teachers *want* to help kids. However, they become jaded when year after year they are told to use programs that are supposed to produce stellar improvements but deliver mediocre results.

It's important to understand that, even if your child were to become a "reading savant" by age five because of your intentional, loving, and successful coaching, you will encounter few educators throughout your child's school years who will welcome what you have to say about what it takes to transform a child into an excellent reader. They will be resistant either because what you share with them contradicts what they "have to do" according to local, state, or federal mandates or because what you have to say contradicts what they "know" to be true about reading. New ideas in any field of endeavor frequently take many years to be accepted. The world-renowned science historian Thomas Kuhn noted that the supporters of old ideas usually have to die before new ideas replace the old!

The best any of us can do is to be prepared with answers as people begin to ask the question, "Interactive constructivism? What's that?" When people start asking questions, it means they are taking the initiative for their own learning. That is exactly what you want to happen. When others express interest in how your child became an excellent reader, they will be ready to hear what you have to say.

Answering Commonly Asked Questions

If you do get an opportunity to discuss the views on reading development and reading presented in this book, it may be helpful to have answers to some questions that thoughtful people commonly ask.

Question: If focusing on identifying words causes reading problems, why doesn't everyone except those who taught themselves to read have a reading problem?

Short Answer: Every child is fully capable of figuring out the reading process for himself, in spite of the type of instruction. Children who teach themselves to read prove this point. The reality of the millions of children from all walks of life who have reading problems demonstrates, however, that not everyone does.

Explanation: Children who teach themselves to read prove that direct instruction is not required for learning. So long as the brain can establish a link between what it already knows and what it is trying to make sense of, it is capable of figuring out nearly anything for itself.

When young children first learn to read in a skills-based program, their reading is typically laborious and painfully slow. In search of a more efficient means to be successful, some children will experiment (below the level of consciousness) with alternative strategies. Some will be successful and find a better way to do business, and some will not. Those who are successful discover on their own that reading and talking are much alike because both require the prediction of meaning.

Once the brain implicitly becomes aware of this relationship, it begins asking sophisticated questions: "How can I keep predictions of the author's message coming?" "How can I make sure I'm predicting the same message the author intended?" "How can I use strategically selected phonics information (sound-symbol relationships that do not involve a left-to-right decoding strategy) to aid in making the predictive strategy work?" These are significantly different questions from this one: "What is that *word*?" The right implicit questions put students on the right path to figuring out the complex process of passage reading for themselves.

Unfortunately, many students do not follow the path to the end because they have not established a true concept of excellence. Their brains may stop when they perceive that their reading is "good enough." These students may score OK on reading achievement tests and do OK in school. But, unless they have strong intent and are willing to work hard, they are unlikely to excel in an academic environment.

It is quite likely that many more adults and children have reading problems than are actually reported. For children in school, only those who score poorly on reading achievement tests or who are failing their classes are identified as having reading problems. Many students whose brains are not producing excellent reading read "well enough" to score in an average range on a reading test. These students tend to be the "B" or "C" students who could be "A" students if they were excellent readers.

Where adults are concerned, at workforce literacy projects in our corporate work, we almost always discover numerous managers, supervisors, engineers, and other highly qualified and well-educated individuals whose brains are not reading correctly. In every case, once tutoring in the interactive constructivist model is completed, they report improved comprehension and more ease and comfort with reading. Almost all report significant changes in reading behavior as well—they read more, read faster, and begin to read for pleasure.

Question: If learning to read through decoding is potentially so harmful, why do some children and teens who learned to read through phonics programs and who used to be struggling readers become great readers without any help from anyone?

Short Answer: Our own intent combined with the fact that our brains are equipped to figure out how to perform nearly any process makes it possible for us to overcome obstacles—including reading difficulties.

Explanation: Some struggling readers will develop an almost obsessive intent to excel at a particular activity—bass fishing, for example. The aspiring fisherman will seek to learn as much as he can from observation and from talking with other bass fishermen, and, one day, he realizes that he can learn more by reading about the subject.

In spite of his significant reading problem, he wants to read magazines and books about bass fishing so that he can learn more about the sport. He works diligently, focusing on the author's message, because he is eager to know about bass fishing. His brain begins to implicitly experiment with new strategies to read more efficiently and effectively. Think about the environment he has created for his brain: he's focused on meaning (and no one is trying to redirect his focus to figuring out the words), he has strong intent to know what the author is saying, and he already knows a lot about bass fishing, so it won't be difficult for his brain to establish links between what he already knows and the information he is reading—the essence of the predictive strategy. In such an environment, it is highly likely that his brain will be successful at figuring out excellent reading.

Question: Are you saying that this is the only way to learn to read?

Short Answer: Not quite. I'm saying that all brains learn to perform processes in fundamentally the same way, and all brains require the same things to learn to perform processes with excellence. If the requirements are met, the brain will learn to perform the process with excellence; if they are not met, excellent reading ability will not develop.

Explanation: To figure out how to perform a process well, the brain has to perform these functions:

1. Establish a concept of excellence for passage reading that will be a yardstick for performance.
2. Maintain strong intent to achieve excellence.
3. Engage consistently in an implicit cycle of prediction geared to figuring out how to read with excellence.

Any reading program that is designed to provide for these requirements will be effective in helping students become excellent readers.

Question: How do you explain why some children's reading problems are successfully addressed through skills-based programs?

Short Answer: Whether any program is able to "successfully address reading problems" depends on the expectation established for participants. With interactive constructivist methodology, we expect students' reading problems to be totally eliminated, meaning the students can read with comfort and understand anything they freely choose to read. Other programs expect improvement in word-identification skills, vocabulary, fluency, and comprehension, but they expect the improvement to be incremental, and they do not necessarily expect to completely eliminate the reading problem.

Explanation: Imagine a boy in second grade who is a total nonreader. Then imagine that he goes into a skills-based reading intervention program geared to helping him become better at identifying words. The program produces a measure of success because it is well designed and the teacher is terrific.

The student becomes better at identifying words. Now he can read second-grade materials, but it's tough for him. He has to work hard to read, his reading is slow and laborious, and his comprehension is not very good, but he *can* read and he couldn't before. What do you think his parents will say? Was the program successful in addressing his reading problems? What will his teacher say? All will agree that the program was successful, even though the second-grader still has a severe reading problem as evidenced by the considerable effort he continues to expend while reading and by his limited comprehension.

School personnel frequently tell me that they are very satisfied with the results of a particular reading program that they have brought into their schools. When I probe further, however, they also tell me that the program doesn't work very well for special-education-qualified students or the Title I students they serve, and it really isn't working with kids who do not speak English as their first language. Then they acknowledge that the Native American students in their school are performing poorly in reading, and the African American kids aren't doing much better. So, *why* are they satisfied with the results of the program?

The answer hurts my heart. School personnel don't *expect* students who are failing to become excellent readers or to even do much better than the level they've already attained. It isn't that they don't *want* to help them. If they knew what to do, they'd do it. However, year after year of trying different programs has told them that there isn't any way to help these kids. See the vicious circle? If you don't expect kids to improve much, then you will be satisfied with a program that doesn't get good results. And, if you're satisfied with a program that isn't getting good results, then you won't be looking for one that will.

Reading Problems Are Not the Fault of Children, Parents, or Schools

As we have seen in this book, reading problems are not the fault of children, or parents, or schools. Reading problems are the fault of old ideas about reading that do not accurately reflect what the brain requires to read with excellence.

The current movement in education to hold teachers and school administrators accountable for their schools' reading test scores has brought the focus of classroom instruction back to the individual skills commonly associated with reading—skills that represent views of reading similar to those held by "experts" *two hundred years ago.*

The interactive constructivist view represents a revolution in thinking—a new view grounded in the rapidly increasing knowledge of how we can focus mental force to change our own brains. If you have faithfully adhered to the interactive constructivist techniques suggested in this book, *you* are choosing your child's reading path. You are choosing to nudge your child gently in the direction of constructing his own intelligence through a mind-shaping process of establishing a high standard of excellence and using a predictive strategy that will cause him to experiment and make implicit discoveries about how to make excellent reading happen.

Adhere strictly to this view and not only will you ensure your child's reading success, but also you may become a revolutionary! Spread the word: *reading theory is broken*—not children, or parents, or schools.

Appendix
Recommended Books for Children

Simple ABC Books

A to Z. Sandra Boynton. Little Simon, 1984.

ABC and 123: A Sesame Street Treasury of Words. Children's
Television Workshop. Random House, 1998.

Barbie ABC Board Book. Rebecca Knowles. DK Publishing,
2002.

Dr. Seuss's ABC. Dr. Seuss. Random House Books for Young
Readers, 1960.

Gyo Fujikawa's A to Z Picture Book. Grosset & Dunlap, 1974.

My Big Alphabet Book. FunFax. Dorling Kindersley, 1999.

My First ABC Board Book. Helen Melville. DK Publishing, 1999.

My First ABC Play Book. Deborah Lock. DK Publishing, 2003.

ABC Read-Aloud Books

A—My Name Is Alice. Jane Bayer and Steven Kellogg. Puffin
Books, 1987.

ABC: A Child's First Alphabet Book. Alison Jay. Dutton's Children's Books, 2003.

Animalia. Graeme Base. Harry N. Abrams, 1987.

Wordless and Almost Wordless Picture Books

The Angel and the Soldier Boy. Peter Collington. Alfred E. Knopf, 1987.

Anno's Journey. Mitsumasa Anno. Putnam Publishing Group, 1997.

Carl Series (books about Carl the Rottweiler). Alexandra Day.

> *Carl Goes Shopping.* Farrar, Straus & Giroux, 1992 (board ed.).
>
> *Carl's Birthday.* Farrar, Straus & Giroux, 1997 (board ed.).
>
> *Carl's Christmas.* Farrar, Straus & Giroux, 1990 (board ed.); HarperFestival, 1995.
>
> *Good Dog, Carl.* Little Simon, 1996 (board ed.).

First Snow: A Wordless Picture Book. Emily Arnold McCully. Trophy, 1988 (reprint).

Frog Series. Mercer Mayer.

> *A Boy, a Dog, a Frog, and a Friend.* Puffin Books, 1993.
>
> *A Boy, a Dog, and a Frog.* Puffin Books, 1979 (reissue).
>
> *Frog Goes to Dinner.* Puffin Books, 1977.
>
> *Frog on His Own.* Puffin Books, 1991 (reprint).
>
> *Frog, Where Are You?* Puffin Books, 1980.
>
> *One Frog Too Many.* Puffin Books, 1992.

The Grey Lady and the Strawberry Snatcher. Molly Bang. Simon & Schuster Children's Publishing, 1984.

The Hunter and the Animals. Tomie dePaola. Holiday House, 1981.

Is It Red? Is It Yellow? Is It Blue? Tana Hoban. Greenwillow Books, 1987.

Little Star. Antonin Louchard. Hyperion, 2003.

Looking Down. Steve Jenkins. Houghton Mifflin, 2003 (reprint).

The Midnight Adventures of Kelly, Dot, and Esmeralda. John S. Goodall. Margaret K. McElderry, 1999 (reissue).

Noah's Ark. Peter Spier. Doubleday Books for Young Readers, 1977.

On Christmas Eve. Peter Collington. Knopf Books for Young Readers, 1990 (reissue).

Paddy Pork's Holiday. John S. Goodall. Atheneum, 1976.

Pancakes for Breakfast. Tomie dePaola. Voyager Books, 1990 (reissue).

Peter Spier's Rain. Peter Spier. Sagebrush Bound, 1999.

Rosie's Walk. Pat Hutchins. Aladdin, 1971.

The Secret in the Dungeon. Fernando Krahn. Houghton Mifflin, 1983.

The Snowman. Raymond Briggs. Random House Books for Young Readers, 1978.

The Surprise Picnic. John S. Goodall. Margaret K. McElderry, 1999.

Up a Tree. Ed Young. HarperCollins, 1991 (reissue).

Window. Jeannie Baker. Greenwillow Books, 1991.

The Yellow Umbrella. Henrik Drescher. Atheneum, 1987.

Highly Predictable Books

Animal Babies. Bobbie Hamsa. Children's Press, A Rookie Reader, 1985.

Animal Babies. Peter Sloan and Sheryl Sloan. Sagebrush Bound, 2001.

Animal Habitats. Peter Sloan and Sheryl Sloan. Sagebrush Bound, 2001.

Animals I Like to Feed. Peter Sloan and Sheryl Sloan. Sagebrush Bound, 2001.

At the Farm. Peter Sloan, Sheryl Sloan, and Gali Weiss. Sagebrush Bound, 2001.

At the Zoo. Peter Sloan and Sheryl Sloan. Sagebrush Bound, 2001.

Beach Day. Mercer Mayer. Mercer Mayer First Readers, 2001.

Big Mammals. Peter Sloan and Sheryl Sloan. Sagebrush Bound, 2001.

Breakfast with John. Janice Boland and Joe Veno. Richard C. Owen Publishers, 1997.

Building Things. Brian Cutting. Wright Group/McGraw-Hill, 1988.

Cat Tails. Kittie Boss and Erin Marie Mauterer. Richard C. Owen Publishers, 1999.

Flying and Floating. Peter Sloan, Sheryl Sloan, and T. Culkin-Lawrence. Sagebrush Bound, 2001.

Game Day. Cari Meister. Sagebrush Bound, 2002.

I Went to the Beach. Lori Morgan. Richard C. Owen Publishers, 2001.

Is It Floating? Fred and Jeanne Biddulph. Wright Group, 1992.

It Looked Like Spilt Milk. Charles G. Shaw. HarperTrophy, 1988 (reprint).

The Lion and the Mouse. Gail Herman. Random House Books for Young Readers, 1998.

Little and Big. Peter Sloan and Sheryl Sloan. Sagebrush Bound, 2001.

Moving. Peter Sloan and Sheryl Sloan. Sagebrush Bound, 2001.

On Vacation. Peter Sloan, Sheryl Sloan, and Pat Reynolds. Sagebrush Bound, 2001.

Pigs Peek. Rhonda Cox. Richard C. Owen Publishers, 1996.

The Strongest Animal. Janice Boland and Gary Torrisi. Richard C. Owen Publishers, 1996.

Transportation Museum. Peter Sloan, Sheryl Sloan, and Pat Reynolds. Sagebrush Bound, 2001.

A Tree Fell over the River. Peter Sloan, Sheryl Sloan, and T. Culkin-Lawrence. Sagebrush Bound, 2001.

What Animals Eat. Peter Sloan and Sheryl Sloan. Sagebrush Bound, 2001.

What Comes Out at Night. Peter Sloan and Sheryl Sloan. Sagebrush Bound, 2001.

World Around Us. Peter Sloan and Sheryl Sloan. Sagebrush Bound, 2001.

Predictable Books

Alligator Shoes. Arthur Dorros. Puffin Books, 1992 (revised).

Big Brown Bear. David McPhail. Green Light Readers, 2003.

Big Machines. Peter Sloan and Sheryl Sloan. Sagebrush Bound, 2001.

Biscuit Finds a Friend. Alyssa Satin Capucilli. HarperTrophy, 1998.

Goldilocks and the Three Bears. Betty Miles and Bari Weissman. Aladdin, 1998.

Henry. Donna Beveridge and Brock Nicol. Richard C. Owen
   Publishers, 1999.
I Love Rocks. Cari Meister. Children's Press, Rookie Readers,
   2001.
Katydids. Nic Bishop. Richard C. Owen Publishers, 1998.
New York City Buildings. Ann Mace. Richard C. Owen Pub-
   lishers, 1997.
Parts of a Bike. Peter Sloan and Sheryl Sloan. Sagebrush
   Bound, 2001.
Tiny the Snow Dog. Cari Meister. Sagebrush Bound, 2003.
Tiny's Bath. Cari Meister. Puffin Books, 1999.

Minimal-Print Early Readers

And I Mean It, Stanley. Crosby Bonsall. HarperTrophy, 1984.
Andi's Wool. Rhonda Cox. Richard C. Owen Publishers, 1997.
At the Horse Show. Rhonda Cox. Richard C. Owen Publishers,
   1997.
Big Dog, Little Dog. P. D. Eastman. Random House Books for
   Young Readers, 1973.
The Cat Family. Christine Butterworth and Donna Bailey.
   Steck-Vaughn, 1990.
Clifford the Big Red Dog. Norman Bridwell. Scholastic, 1997.
Clouds. Brian Cutting and Jillian Cutting. Wright Group,
   1989.
Drawbridge. Richard Latta. Richard C. Owen Publishers, 1997.
The Hermit Crab. Brian Cutting and Jillian Cutting. Wright
   Group/McGraw-Hill, 1988.
Just for You. Mercer Mayer. Demco Media, 1975.
No Dogs Allowed. Suzanne Hardin and Joanne Friar. Richard
   C. Owen Publishers, 1997.
Powwow. Rhonda Cox. Richard C. Owen Publishers, 2001.
Shells. Betsy Franco. Sagebrush Bound, 2001.
Small World. Brian Cutting and Jillian Cutting. Wright
   Group/McGraw-Hill, 1988.
The Sparrows. Robert Slaughter. Robert C. Owen Publishers,
   1997.

Spiders Everywhere. Betty L. Baker and Judith Pfeiffer. Richard
 C. Owen Publishers, 1997.

Turtle Nest. Lola M. Schaeffer and Neesa Becker. Richard C.
 Owen Publishers, 1996.

Underwater Journey. Brian Cutting and Jillian Cutting. Wright
 Group/McGraw-Hill, 1988.

When Tiny Was Tiny. Cari Meister and Rich Davis. Puffin
 Books, 1999.

Why the Frog Has Big Eyes. Betsy Franco and Joung Un Kim.
 Green Light Readers, 2003 (reissue).

Resource Books

*The Newbery and Caldecott Awards: A Guide to the Medal and
 Honor Books.* American Library Association, 2004.

The Read-Aloud Handbook. 4th ed. Jim Trelease. Penguin
 Books, 2001.

Selected References

Chapter 1

Adams, M. J. 1990. *Beginning to Read*. Cambridge, MA: MIT Press.

———. 1998. *Beginning to Read: Thinking and Learning About Print*. 10th ed. Cambridge, MA: MIT Press.

Allman, W. F. 1989. *Apprentices of Wonder: Inside the Neural Network Revolution*. New York: Bantam Books.

Chall, J. S., V. A. Jacobs, and L. E. Baldwin. 1990. *The Reading Crisis: Why Poor Children Fall Behind*. Cambridge, MA: Harvard University Press.

Durkin, D. 1965. *Phonics and the Teaching of Reading*. 2nd ed. New York: Bureau of Publications, Teachers College, Columbia University.

———. 1966. *Children Who Read Early*. New York: Teachers College Press.

Gaffney, J. S., and R. C. Anderson. 2000. "Trends in Reading Research in the United States: Changing Intellectual Currents over Three Decades." In *Handbook of Reading Research*, vol. 3, ed. M. L. Kamil, P. B. Mosenthal, P. D. Pearson, and R. Barr. Mahwah, NJ: Lawrence Erlbaum Associates.

Goodman, K. S., ed. 1968. *The Psycholinguistic Nature of the Reading Process.* Detroit: Wayne State University Press.

Hall, S. L., and L. C. Moats. 1999. *Straight Talk About Reading.* Chicago: Contemporary Books.

Hebb, D. O. 1966. *A Textbook of Psychology.* Philadelphia: Saunders.

Inhelder, B., and J. Piaget. 1964. *The Early Growth of Logic in the Child.* New York: Harper & Row.

International Dyslexia Association. 2003. *Annals of Dyslexia 2003* (53).

Johnson, G. 1992. *In the Palaces of Memory.* New York: Vintage Books.

Kohler, I. 1964. *The Formation and Transformation of the Perceptual World.* Vol. 3 of *Psychological Issues.* Monograph 12. Vienna: International University Press.

LeDoux, J. 2002. *Synaptic Self: How Our Brains Become Who We Are.* New York: Penguin Books.

Lyon, G. R. 2003. "The Critical Need for Evidence-Based Comprehensive and Effective Early Childhood Programs." Testimony to the U.S. Senate Committee on Health, Education, Labor, and Pensions hearing; *Reauthorizing Head Start: Preparing Children to Succeed in School and in Life.* July 22.

———. 2003. "MacNeil/Lehrer NewsHour"; excerpt from interview: ". . . only 20 percent of teachers are effective in reading instruction." June 2.

National Institute for Child Health and Human Development. 2002. Request for Applications: HD-03-012; release date: Dec. 19, 2003.

National Reading Panel. 2000. *Report of the National Reading Panel: Teaching Children to Read.* Washington, DC: National Institute of Child Health and Human Development.

National Research Council. 1998. *Preventing Reading Difficulties in Young Children.* Washington, DC: National Academy Press.

Piaget, J. 1950. *The Psychology of Intelligence.* Trans. M. Piercy and D. E. Berlyne. London: Routledge.

Shaywitz, S. E. 2003. *Overcoming Dyslexia.* New York: Knopf.

Smith, F. 1978. *Understanding Reading: A Psycholinguistic Analysis of Reading and Learning to Read.* 2nd ed. New York: Holt, Rinehart, & Winston.

Stainthorp, R., and D. Hughes. 1999. *Learning from Children Who Read at an Early Age.* London: Routledge.

Chapter 2

Adams, M. J. 1990. *Beginning to Read.* Cambridge, MA: MIT Press.

Dooling, D. J., and R. Lachman. 1971. "Effects of Comprehension on Retention of Prose." *Journal of Experimental Psychology* 88: 216–22.

Fisher, D. E., and W. L. Shebilske. 1985. "There Is More That Meets the Eye Than the Eye Mind Assumption." *In Eye Movements and Human Information Processing*, ed. R. Groner, G. W. McConkie, and C. Menz, 149–57. Amsterdam: Elsevier Science Publishers.

Goodman, K., and C. L. Burke. 1973. "Theoretically Based Studies of Patterns of Miscues in Oral Reading Performance." Final Report. Project OEG-0-9-320375-4269. Washington, DC: U.S. Office of Education.

Goodman, K. S. 1964. "The Linguistics of Reading." *Elementary School Journal* 64 (7): 359.

Goodman, K. S., ed. 1968. *The Psycholinguistic Nature of the Reading Process.* Detroit: Wayne State University Press.

Just, M. A., and P. A. Carpenter. 1984. "Using Eye Fixations to Study Reading Comprehension." In *New Methods*

in Reading Comprehension Research, ed. D. E. Kieras
and M. A. Just, 151–82. Hillsdale, NJ: Lawrence
Erlbaum Associates.

Keller, T. A., P. A. Carpenter, and M. A. Just. 2001. "The
Neural Bases of Sentence Comprehension: A fMRI
Examination of Syntactic and Lexical Processing."
Cerebral Cortex 11 (3): 223–37.

Lavigne, F., and S. Denis. 2002. "Neural Network Modeling
of Learning of Contextual Constraints on Adaptive
Anticipations." *International Journal of Computing
Anticipatory Systems* 12.

McGuinness, Diane. 1997. *Why Our Children Can't Read and
What We Can Do About It: A Scientific Revolution in
Reading*. New York: The Free Press.

Miller, G. A. 1956. "The Magical Number Seven, Plus or
Minus Two: Some Limits on Our Capacity for
Processing Information. *Psychological Review* 63:
81–97.

National Research Council. 1998. *Preventing Reading
Difficulties in Young Children*. Washington, DC:
National Academy Press.

O'Regan, J. K. 1981. "The Convenient Viewing Position
Hypothesis." In *Eye Movements, Cognition, and Visual
Perception*, ed. D. F. Fisher, R. A. Monty, and J. W.
Senders, 289–98. Hillsdale, NJ: Lawrence Erlbaum
Associates.

O'Regan, J. K., A. Levy-Schoen, J. Pynte, and B. Brugaillere.
1984. "Convenient Fixation Location Within Isolated
Words of Different Length and Structure." *Journal of
Experimental Psychology: Human Perception and
Performance* 10: 250–57.

Paulson, E. J., and A. E. Freeman. 2003. *Insight from the
Eyes*. Portsmouth, NH: Heinemann.

Plaut, D., J. McClelland, M. Seidenberg, and K. Patterson.
1996. "Understanding Normal and Impaired Word
Reading: Computational Principles in Quasi-Regular
Domains." *Psychological Review* 103: 56–115.

Price, C. J., and J. T. Devlin. 2003. "The Myth of the Visual Word Form Area." *NeuroImage* 19, Comments and Controversies, 473–81.

Price, C. J., D. Winterburn, A. L. Giraud, C. J. Moore, and U. Noppeney. 2003. "Cortical Localization of the Visual and Auditory Word Form Areas: A Reconsideration of the Evidence." *Brain and Language* 86 (2): 272–86.

Rumelhart, D., and J. McClelland. 1986. *Parallel Distributed Processing*. Vol. 1. Cambridge, MA: MIT Press.

Rumelhart, D. E. 1977. "Toward an Interactive Model of Reading." In *Attention and Performance*, vol 6, ed. S. Dornic. Hillsdale, NJ: Lawrence Erlbaum Associates.

———. 1980. "Schemata: The Building Blocks of Cognition." In *Theoretical Issues in Reading Comprehension*, ed. R. Spiro, B. Bruce, and W. Brewer. Hillsdale, NJ: Lawrence Erlbaum Associates.

Seidenberg, M., and J. McClelland. 1989. "A Distributed, Developmental Model of Word Recognition and Naming." *Psychological Review* 96: 523–68.

Shaywitz, S. E. 2003. *Overcoming Dyslexia*. New York: Knopf.

Smith, F. 1975. *Comprehension and Learning: A Conceptual Framework for Teachers*. New York: Holt, Rinehart, & Winston.

———. 1978. *Understanding Reading: A Psycholinguistic Analysis of Reading and Learning to Read*. 2nd ed. New York: Holt, Rinehart, & Winston.

Stevens, M., and M. Grainger. 2003. "Letter Visibility and the Viewing Position Effect in Visual Word Recognition." *Perception and Psychophysics* 65 (1): 133–51.

Tadlock, D. R. 2004. *Interactive Constructivism and Reading: The Nature of Neural Networks Challenges the Phonological Processing Hypothesis*. Unpublished. Available at cost at readright.com or by calling (360) 427-9440.

Vandenberghe, R., A. C. Nobre, and C. J. Price. 2002. "The Response of Left Temporal Cortex to Sentences." *Journal of Cognitive Neuroscience* 14: 550–60.

Chapter 3

Allman, W. F. 1989. *Apprentices of Wonder: Inside the Neural Network Revolution.* New York: Bantam Books.

Ames, J. 1997. *Mastery: Interviews with 30 Remarkable People.* Portland, OR: Rudra Press.

Baddeley, A. 1987. *Working Memory.* Oxford: Oxford University Press.

Baddeley, A. D., and G. J. Hitch. 1974. "Working Memory." In *The Psychology of Learning and Motivation: Advances in Research and Theory*, vol. 8, ed. G. H. Bower, 47–90. New York: Academic Press.

Borkowski, J. G., and J. E. Burke. 1996. "Theories, Models, and Measurements of Executive Functioning." In *Attention, Memory, and Executive Function*, ed. G. R. Lyon and N. A. Krasnegor, 235–61. Baltimore: Paul H. Brookes.

Denckla, M. B. 1995. "A Theory and Model of Executive Function: A Neuropsychological Perspective." In *Attention, Memory, and Executive Function*, ed. G. R. Lyon and N. A. Krasnegor, 263–78. Baltimore: Paul H. Brookes.

Ericsson, K. A. 1996. *The Road to Excellence: The Acquisition of Expert Performance in the Arts and Sciences, Sports, and Games.* Mahwah, NJ: Lawrence Erlbaum Associates.

———. 2002. "Attaining Excellence from Deliberate Practice: Insights from the Study of Expert Performance." In *The Pursuit of Excellence in Education*, ed. M. Ferrari, 21–55. Hillsdale, NJ: Erlbaum.

Godefroy, O. 2003. "Frontal Syndrome and Disorders of Executive Functions." *Journal of Neurology* 250:1–6.

Hebb, D. O. 1949. *The Organization of Behavior.* New York: John Wiley.

Inhelder, B., and J. Piaget. 1964. *The Early Growth of Logic in the Child.* New York: Harper & Row.

Johnson, G. 1992. *In the Palaces of Memory.* New York: Vintage Books.

Kampwirth, T. J., and M. Bates. 1980. "Modality Preference and Teaching Method: A Review of the Research." *Academic Therapy* 15: 597–605.

Laughlin, S. B., and T. J. Sejnowski. 2003. "Communication in Neuronal Networks (A Review)." *Science* 301, Sept. 26: 1870–74.

LeDoux, J. 2002. *Synaptic Self: How Our Brains Become Who We Are*. New York: Penguin Books.

Lynch, G. 1986. *Synapses, Circuits, and the Beginning of Memory*. Cambridge, MA: MIT Press.

Ratey, J. J. 2001. *A User's Guide to the Brain: Perception, Attention, and the Four Theaters of the Brain*. New York: Pantheon Books.

Robinson, H. M. 1972. "Visual and Auditory Modalities Related to Methods for Beginning Reading." *Reading Research Quarterly* 8: 7–39.

Schacter, D., and P. Graf. 1986. "Effects of Elaborative Processing on Implicit and Explicit Memory for New Associations." *Journal of Experimental Psychology: Learning, Memory, and Cognition* 12 (3): 432–44.

Smith, N. V., I. M. Tsimpli, and N. Smith. 1995. *The Mind of a Savant: Language, Learning, and Modularity*. Oxford: Blackwell Publishers.

Stahl, S. A. 1988. "Is There Evidence to Support Matching Reading Styles and Initial Reading Methods? A Reply to Carbo." *Phi Delta Kappan* 70, 317–22.

Tadlock, D. R. 2004. *Interactive Constructivism and Reading: The Nature of Neural Networks Challenges the Phonological Processing Hypothesis*. Unpublished. Available at cost at readright.com or by calling (360) 427-9440.

Chapter 4

Ames, J. 1997. *Mastery: Interviews with 30 Remarkable People*. Portland, OR: Rudra Press.

Ericcson, K. A. 1996. *The Road to Excellence: The Acquisition of Expert Performance in the Arts and Sciences, Sports, and Games*. Mahwah, NJ: Lawrence Erlbaum Associates.

Inhelder, B., and J. Piaget. 1964. *The Early Growth of Logic in the Child*. New York: Harper & Row.

Piaget, J. 1950. *The Psychology of Intelligence*. Trans. M. Piercy and D. E. Berlyne. London: Routledge.

Piaget, J., and B. Inhelder. 1969. *The Psychology of the Child*. New York: Basic Books.

Tadlock, D. R. 1978. "SQ3R: Why It Works, Based on an Information Processing Theory of Learning." *Journal of Reading*, Nov.

Chapter 5

Goodman, K., and C. L. Burke. 1973. "Theoretically Based Studies of Patterns of Miscues in Oral Reading Performance." Final Report. Project OEG-0-9-320375-4269. Washington, DC: U.S. Office of Education.

Goodman, K. S., ed. 1968. *The Psycholinguistic Nature of the Reading Process*. Detroit: Wayne State University.

Hench, J., W. Lefkon, and P. Van Pelt. 2003. *Designing Disney: Imagineering and the Art of the Show*. New York: Disney Editions.

National Research Council. 1998. *Preventing Reading Difficulties in Young Children*, 53. Washington, DC: National Academy Press.

Piaget, J. 1985. *Equilibration of Cognitive Structures: The Central Problem of Intellectual Development*. Chicago: University of Chicago Press.

Schwartz, J. M., and S. Begley. 2002. *The Mind and the Brain: Neuroplasticity and the Power of Mental Force*. New York: ReganBooks/HarperCollins.

Smith, F. 1978. *Understanding Reading: A Psycholinguistic Analysis of Reading and Learning to Read*. 2nd ed. New York: Holt, Rinehart, & Winston.

Sperry, R. W. 1992. "Turnabout on Consciousness: A Mentalist View." *Journal of Mind and Behavior* 13: 259–80.

Trelease, J. 2001. *The Read-Aloud Handbook*. 4th ed. New York: Penguin.

Chapter 6

Allman, W. F. 1989. *Apprentices of Wonder: Inside the Neural Network Revolution*. New York: Bantam Books.

Baddeley, A. 1987. *Working Memory*. Oxford: Oxford University Press.

Borkowski, J. G., and J. E. Burke. 1996. "Theories, Models, and Measurements of Executive Functioning." In *Attention, Memory, and Executive Function*, ed. G. R. Lyon and N. A. Krasnegor, 235–61. Baltimore: Paul H. Brookes.

Denckla, M. B. 1995. "A Theory and Model of Executive Function: A Neuropsychological Perspective." In *Attention, Memory, and Executive Function*, ed. G. R. Lyon and N. A. Krasnegor , 263–78. Baltimore: Paul H. Brookes.

Dubois, D. M. 1998. "Introduction to Computing Anticipatory Systems." *International Journal of Computing Anticipatory Systems* 2: 3–14.

Hebb, D. O. 1949. *The Organization of Behavior*. New York: John Wiley.

Inhelder, B., and J. Piaget. 1964. *The Early Growth of Logic in the Child*. New York: Harper & Row.

Lavigne, F., and S. Denis. 2002. "Neural Network Modeling of Learning of Contextual Constraints on Adaptive Anticipations." *International Journal of Computing Anticipatory Systems* 12.

LeDoux, J. 2002. *Synaptic Self: How Our Brains Become Who We Are*. New York: Penguin Books.

Chapter 7

Tadlock, D. R. 1978. "SQ3R: Why It Works, Based on an Information Processing Theory of Learning." *Journal of Reading*, Nov.

————. 1986. "A Practical Application of Psycholinguistics and Piaget's Theory to Reading Instruction." *Reading Psychology* 7 (3): 183–95.

————. 2004. *Interactive Constructivism and Reading: The Nature of Neural Networks Challenges the Phonological Processing Hypothesis.* Unpublished. Available at cost at readright.com or by calling (360) 427-9440.

Tadlock, K. R., and D. Tadlock. 2004. READ RIGHT® *Tutor Manual.* (1st ed. 1998.) Shelton, WA: Read Right Systems, Inc.

Chapter 8

AAP/AAPOS/AAO. 1998. "Learning Disabilities, Dyslexia, and Vision: A Joint Statement of the American Academy of Pediatrics, American Association for Pediatric Ophthalmology and Strabismus, and American Academy of Ophthalmology." Joint policy statement.

AOA. 2004. "The Use of Tinted Lenses and Colored Overlays for the Treatment of Dyslexia and Other Related Reading and Learning Disorders." Opinion statement of the American Optometric Association.

Baddeley, A. D., and G. J. Hitch. 1974. "Working Memory." In *The Psychology of Learning and Motivation: Advances in Research and Theory*, vol. 8, ed. G. H. Bower, 47–90. New York: Academic Press.

Bellis, T. J. 2002. *When the Brain Can't Hear: Unraveling the Mystery of Auditory Processing Disorder.* New York: Pocket Books.

Borkowski, J. G., and J. E. Burke. 1996. "Theories, Models, and Measurements of Executive Functioning." In *Attention, Memory, and Executive Function*, ed. G. R. Lyon and N. A. Krasnegor, 235–61. Baltimore: Paul H. Brookes.

Bowan, M. 2002. "Learning Disabilities, Dyslexia, and Vision: A Rebuttal." *Optometry* 73 (9): 553–75.

Bull, R., and G. Scerif. 2001. "Executive Functioning as a Predictor of Children's Mathematics Ability: Inhibition, Switching, and Working Memory." *Developmental Neuropsychology* 19 (3): 273–93.

Butterfield, E. C., and J. M. Belmont. 1977. "Assessing and Improving the Executive Cognitive Functions of Mentally Retarded People." In *Psychological Issues in Mental Retardation*, ed. I. Bialer and M. Sternlicht, 277–318. New York: Psychological Dimensions.

Chall, J. S., V. A. Jacobs, and L. E. Baldwin. 1990. *The Reading Crisis: Why Poor Children Fall Behind.* Cambridge, MA: Harvard University Press.

Foorman, B. R., D. J. Francis, D. M. Novy, and D. Liberman. 1991. "How Letter-Sound Instruction Mediates Progress in First-Grade Reading and Spelling." *Journal of Educational Psychology* 83: 456–69.

Hall, S. L., and L. C. Moats. 1999. *Straight Talk About Reading*, 279. Chicago: Contemporary Books.

Irlen, H. 1991. *Reading by the Colors*. New York: Perigree Books.

Keller, T. A., P. A. Carpenter, and M. A. Just. 2001. "The Neural Bases of Sentence Comprehension: A fMRI Examination of Syntactic and Lexical Processing." *Cerebral Cortex* 11 (3): 223–37.

LeDoux, J. 2002. *Synaptic Self: How Our Brains Become Who We Are.* New York: Penguin Books.

Lovegrove, W. J., A. Bowling, B. Badcock, and M. Blackwood. 1980. "Specific Reading Disability: Differences in Contrast Sensitivity as a Function of Spatial Frequency." *Science* 210: 439–40.

Peterson, S. W., P. T. Fox, M. I. Posner, and M. E. Raichle. 1988. "Positron Emission Tomographic Studies of the Cortical Anatomy of Single-Word Processing. *Nature* 331: 585–89.

Price, C. J., D. Winterburn, A. L. Giraud, C. J. Moore, and U. Noppeney. 2003. "Cortical Localization of the Visual and Auditory Word Form Areas: A Reconsideration of the Evidence." *Brain and Language* 86 (2): 272–86.

Pugh, K., B. A. Shaywitz, S. E. Shaywitz, D. P. Shankweiler, L. Katz, J. M. Fletcher, P. Skudlarski, R. Fulbright, R. Constable, R. Bronen, C. Lacadie, and J. Gore. 1997. "Predicting Reading Performance from Neuroimaging Profiles: The Cerebral Basis of Phonological Effects in Printed Word Identification." *Journal of Experimental Psychology: Human Perception and Performance* 23: 299–318.

Schwartz, J. M., and S. Begley. 2002. *The Mind and the Brain: Neuroplasticity and the Power of Mental Force.* New York: ReganBooks/HarperCollins.

Shaywitz, S. E. 2003. *Overcoming Dyslexia.* New York: Knopf.

Shaywitz, S. E., B. A. Shaywitz, K. R. Pugh, P. Skudlarski, R. K. Fulbright, R. T. Constable, R. A. Bronen, J. M. Fletcher, A. M. Liberman, D. P. Shankweiler, L. Katz, C. Lacadie, K. E. Marchione, and J. C. Gore. 1996. "The Neurobiology of Developmental Dyslexia as Viewed Through the Lens of Functional Magnetic Resonance Imaging Technology." In *Neuroimaging: A Window to the Neurological Foundations of Learning and Behavior in Children*, ed. G. R. Lyon and J. M. Rumsey, 86–87. Baltimore: Paul H. Brookes.

Sperry, R. W. 1992. "Turnabout on Consciousness: A Mentalist View." *Journal of Mind and Behavior* 13: 259–80.

Stanovich, K. E. 1988. "Explaining the Differences Between the Dyslexic and Garden-Variety Poor Reader: The Phonological Core Variable Difference Model." *Journal of Learning Disabilities* 21: 590–604.

Stein, J. 2001. "The Magnocellular Theory of Developmental Dyslexia." *Dyslexia* 7: 12–36.

Stone, R. 2003. *The Light Barrier: Understanding the Mystery of Irlen Syndrome and Light-Based Reading Difficulties.* New York: St. Martin's Press.

Tallal, P. 1980. "Auditory Temporal Perception, Phonics, and Reading Disabilities in Children." *Brain and Language* 9: 182–98.

Vandenberghe, R., A. C. Nobre, and C. J. Price. 2002. "The Response of Left Temporal Cortex to Sentences." *Journal of Cognitive Neuroscience* 14: 550–60.

Wilkins, A. J. 1994. *Visual Stress*. Oxford: Oxford University Press.

Chapter 9

Kuhn, T. S. 1996. *The Structure of Scientific Revolutions*, 3rd ed. Chicago: University of Chicago Press.

Index

ABC read-aloud books
  as book category, 129
  recommended, 195
  technique for using, 132–33
Activities
  for learning the alphabet,
    108–17
  for understanding decoding
    versus passage reading,
    23–25
  for understanding memory
    limitations, 25–27
  for understanding predictive
    strategy, 36–39
  for understanding reading
    from meaning, 27–29
  for understanding visual
    sampling, 32–36
Affirming statements, 90. *See
  also* Praise, false
Age, child's
  brain function and, 46, 47
  reading development and,
    61–62
Alphabet, learning the
  alphabet books for, 108–10
  alphabet games for, 114–17
  refrigerator magnets for,
    112–14
  reliable letters for, 110–12
"Alphabet Song", 120–21
Angelou, Maya, 52
Anticipation
  brain function and, 12–13
  in formula for excellence, 56,
    60
  stories and, 95

Anxiety
  barrier to reading
    development, 88
  coaching and, 152
  concern for reading ability, 180
  intent and, 88
Appreciation for reading, 88
Armstrong, Lance, 83, 85
Audiobooks, 78, 151
Auditory processing, 167–69
Author's experience
  as early reader, 4–5
  as parent and reading expert,
    5–17
Award-winning books, 93, 127,
  200

Barriers to reading development
  brain damage, 162, 175–77
  coaching and, 156–57
  concept of excellence and, 162,
    164–66
  decoding, 39–40, 190
  focus on word identification,
    162, 163–64
  insufficient intent, 87, 162,
    166–67
  intent and anxiety, 88
  processing disturbances, 162,
    167–75
Bedtime stories, 89, 120
Book categories
  ABC read-aloud books, 129,
    132–33, 195
  description of, 129–30, 157
  highly predictable books, 130,
    135–45, 197–98

About the Authors

Dee Tadlock, the developer of the interactive constructivist READ RIGHT program, earned her Ph.D. in reading education in 1978. She has taught reading at every level from elementary school through college and has also worked with adult literacy in community college, community-based, and workforce literacy programs. She is currently director of Research and Development for READ RIGHT Systems, Inc., a company she cofounded in 1991 to bring the READ RIGHT methodology to struggling readers in elementary, middle, and high schools and in corporations.

Rhonda Stone is a former journalist and parent advocate for reading issues. She has worked in both education, as a public information specialist, and health care, as a grant writer. She first became acquainted with Dee Tadlock when her children developed reading problems in spite of a home-based emphasis on phonics and learning decoding skills. The discovery that both of her children have a form of light-sensitivity that causes problems in classroom situations surprised her and started her on a journey to understand why visual processing issues are ignored as a threat to reading development. Her first book is called *The Light Barrier* (St. Martin's Press, 2003).

Four products and services are available through READ RIGHT® Systems, Inc.

1. READ RIGHT **Early Reader Kit** includes a collection of books appropriate for preschoolers and nonreaders: a mix of alphabet books, picture books, highly predictable books, predictable books, and minimal-print early readers.
2. READ RIGHT **Long-Distance Telephone Tutoring Services** are offered at a per-session cost similar to that of other national tutoring programs.
3. READ RIGHT **School and Industrial Programs** for improving reading and English communication skills are explained in information packets, which will be sent upon request to schools, corporations, and small businesses.
4. **An Academic Paper** explaining the interactive constructivist view of reading and reading development is available for printing, shipping, and handling costs.

For information on any of these products and services, see the READ RIGHT website at readright.com or call (360) 427-9440.